PREFACE

During a recent visit to the United States I was privileged to address patient audiences in four seminaries on subjects which the following pages are concerned with. I visited the Baptist Seminary at Covina, California, the Associated Mennonite Seminaries at Goshen and Elkhart, Indiana, and the Southern Baptist Seminaries at New Orleans and at Louisville. What you will read in the following pages is an expansion of the Drexel Lectures at Covina, of the Gheens Lectures at Louisville, and of similar but less grandiloquently named courses at the other two places. What I actually said in these places varied as I went from one to another; I found myself altering, and then wholly abandoning, the scripts I had prepared. The subsequent friendly discussions with my audiences taught me a great deal, some of which I have tried to incorporate in this book.

Now that I have come to write it down, what I think you have here is the record of conversation between an Englishman and some Americans. I am most anxious that nobody should think I was laying down the law. We are dealing here with a subject upon which even the efficient administrations of the U.S.A. have hardly touched at any depth. The conversation is still wide open. If I suggest that Americans have much to learn, I hasten to add that Britons have more, and that I myself ha

I cannot help ⸻ ⸻ ⸻ nt to mention by name o ⸻ ⸻ om I have, as it were, imag ⸻ ⸻ hammered this out on my ⸻ es Mitchell, professor of m ⸻ moment I regard Bob Mitchell as ⸻ e American side of this dialogue.

3

You know what the dialogue is. On the one hand, there is a tendency among Americans to claim that religion in Britain is in a very poor way. This, while I always resist statements that imply it, I take to be a form of neighborly compassion. British churches are far less well peopled than American ones, and British ministers, at any rate in the dissenting denominations, are very much less well supported materially by their congregations than American ministers. Indeed, the aspect of British religion that strikes any American visitor is of dowdy and impoverished inefficiency. More than anybody, the musician feels this.

On the other hand, it is common form for the Englishman who visits America to come back and say that religion there is big business, that it is (I learned this phrase, as so many others of its kind, from Bob Mitchell) "an inch thick and a mile wide." We come back to our 2,500 dollars a year and congratulate ourselves on being poor as church mice and about as attractive.

Now the American who comes into my dimly lit and thinly peopled church and thinks it is a deadfall is a snob. And the Englishman who thinks American religion has no depth is a snob.

We get on better when Englishmen see that, at least in some places, American religion has an astonishing distinction and sensitiveness, and when Americans see that in some places British religion is really in fighting form—if it is at present fighting with weapons no better than Churchill's "bottles on the beaches." We get on better because we are polite to each other and at least ready to listen.

But Bob Mitchell, when we met on this side of the Atlantic, took this further. He it was who, when I defended the dowdiness and ineptitude and tried to say that it wasn't the whole story, took away a copy of Gibson Winter's *The Suburban Captivity of the Church* and came back saying, "That's just not true!" He really pressed me on the dimness of British religion. He said that if suburban churches in America were getting the people they were doing a job, and who was Winter, or who was I, to try to sell them short?

Well, that was that. But later I was to see this Mitchell on his own ground. What was he doing? Telling everybody in the neighborhood of Los Angeles that they were all doing fine?

ERIK ROUTLEY

MUSIC
LEADERSHIP
IN
THE
CHURCH

A Conversation Chiefly with My American
Friends

NASHVILLE   ABINGDON (♪) PRESS   NEW YORK

MUSIC LEADERSHIP IN THE CHURCH

Copyright © 1967 by Abingdon Press

Library of Congress Catalog Card Number: 67-14992

Chapter 7 is reprinted by permission from *Journal of Church
Music,* December, 1966 and January, 1967. Copyright by Fortress
Press, Philadelphia. Chapter 6 is reprinted by permission of
Epworth Press from *Mosaic,* October, 1965.

SET UP, PRINTED, AND BOUND BY THE
PARTHENON PRESS, AT NASHVILLE,
TENNESSEE, UNITED STATES OF AMERICA

Filling them up with gospel songs and barbershop liturgies? Preaching complacency? Oh, no. Making use of his astonishing skill and alertness in his chosen trade of teacher and choirmaster, he was summoning the choirmasters from small and (yes, it is possible in America) struggling churches and playing them tapes of Tippett's *Magnificat* and Krenek's electronic cantata, Malcolm Williamson's *Procession of Palms* and Zimmermann's *Psalmkonzert*. He was taking these people up the hill and showing them the view and making them feel that life was worthwhile. He was making them sightsing contemporary church music of the kind they could take straight back to their churches. And he was doing this for theological students and for ministers of music.

No doubt there are scores of men doing this. I did indeed meet enough musicians of distinction to be able to see that in some parts of the U.S.A., at any rate, this business is a lot more than an inch thick. I met the high-grade musical tradition of Southern Methodist University under Lloyd Pfautsch and Carlton Young. I saw what Dr. Mary Oyer is doing for music among the Indiana Mennonites—and her contribution of sensitiveness and scholarship to that tradition is going to be historic. I encountered the most exciting and (I have to confess) unexpected liberality of the Southern Baptists. (How ignorant and provincial can you get? These people have a great deal more than the Billy Graham *Song Book* to their credit, and I never knew it until I met them.) I even saw some great piles of *The Methodist Hymnal* in production at Abingdon Press.

But I'm dedicating this, for what it may be worth, to Bob Mitchell, because at present he represents the minister of music to me. He doesn't work with the massive and sophisticated equipment that some have, or with the thousands of students that some meet. What he does is turn an ordinary job into a systematic inspiration. I should like to think that a few things said in these pages may help others do that. Because he doesn't need any of it, in the coals-to-Newcastle tradition of dedications, I am offering this to him, with a profound sense of gratitude. If any of the rest of you want a share in it, come and help yourselves.

The material in chapter 6 substantially appeared in the journal *Mosaic* for October, 1965, and that in chapter 7 in the *Journal of Church Music* for December, 1966 and January, 1967. I wish to thank the Reverend Gordon Wakefield, editor of the Epworth Press, and Miss Helen Pfatteicher, editor of the *Journal of Church Music,* for permission to reprint this material here.

E. R.
Edinburgh
June, 1966

CONTENTS

I
THE CHURCH MUSICIAN AND HISTORY

1
Our Neighbors of Other Days

Why History? [1]

Why begin with history? Because nobody can live without his neighbors, and history brings us into contact with our neighbors in time, as the social sciences bring us into touch with our neighbors in space. In Europe we are just emerging from an era during which history has been a subject highly respected. That era was an era of reaction against a previous one in which history was subject to all kinds of romantic perversions —in which, historically, you almost believed what you wanted to believe. And that era in turn reacted against one in which men were much taken up with present realities, with the new dimensions of exploration which new kinds of science and learning had opened up. In our own time we are witnessing in Europe a reaction against "history for its own sake" which is, in the arts and in philosophy and in social studies, tending to emphasize the present and the immediate future at the expense of history. And history has during the past thirty years moved with such speed, and such violence, that the new generation, which in America speaks with so assured a voice, is quite remarkably unwilling to consider history at all.

What has just been said is a sketch of "the history of history." It is a reminder of how people's attitude to history changes from one generation to another. But however attitudes change, what you can never deny without insanity is that history is *there*. People did live in the nineteenth century and in the fourteenth century. So far as what they did is on record, the record is there for you to use. And in times so violently and vertiginously changing as ours, it is worth remembering how G. K. Chesterton once warned us against the attitude of the man who says, "Here is a gate across the road: I do not know why it is there, so I will remove it." Another way of saying the same thing, perhaps a more positive way, is to say that we all need one another, and that we need our forebears just as much as we need our spatial neighbors. They without us cannot, as Hebrews says, be made perfect, but in another sense we are much the better for acknowledging our need of them. These are days in which social studies are pursued with great energy, and in which "togetherness" is much extolled. There is, as I see it, little purpose in talking loudly about togetherness and in projecting social studies of ever-increasing statistical minuteness while one totally ignores all that can be learned from the past.

In church music, anyhow, there are abundant signs that the one thing we need is to compare notes with the people of the past. There are quite a number of gates across the road which people want to remove without finding out why they were put there. There is much talk on both sides of the Atlantic of scrapping almost everything that is familiar in religious observance—of doing away with sermons, of abolishing hymn singing, of pulling down church buildings—which does not show much knowledge of why these things ever came to be part of our accepted custom.[2] But on the other hand, there are some curious growths in our church life, especially among Protestants, whose origin is, if one looks at history, entirely questionable: things that have just settled and grown without any conscious planning or purpose, or things which serve needs whose connection with Christian faith and practice is highly dubious. I shall try to show that a good deal of the confusion that disfigures our church music is the result of impatience with history—of not listening sufficiently to the reasoned speech of our neighbors of the past.

In one way, of course, the church musician cannot avoid using history, however unhistorically minded he may be. For any singing group in any kind of Christian church uses music that comes from many ages. True, it will be one of the points this chapter is designed to make, an adherence to music of one age without due regard to other ages is invariably a sign of weakness, which may point to an underlying theological weakness, in that group's outlook. But however exclusive and sectarian a group may be, it will be found to be singing

10

at least some music that comes from an age other than its specially favored one.

Early Days

What does history, then, tell us about the church musician's work? Let us take some brief excerpts from the story and see.

For much more than a thousand years after the church's foundation, church music was more or less rigidly controlled by the needs of church worship; since the church's ideal during the whole of that period was a sacred society in spiritual control of the whole of Europe, the church's ideal for church music was that it should be the best music available. But by "best" it was obliged to mean most closely conformed to the church's discipline. The notions of "sacred" and "secular" were very clear cut in those days; but although questions were often raised about the relation between the two, the general assumption throughout the area which the church controlled was that in most matters the secular should be under the control of the sacred.

This is a large generalization to which in a full-length history we should have to notice many significant exceptions. The history books do, and they can be easily referred to.[3] There was, of course, secular music long before there was what we call sacred music, because the church comes on the scene relatively late in man's history. There was music long before there was a church, and although some of it was associated with religion, not all of it was. There was secular music running in parallel with the church's music, and the relation between the two for the first thousand years or so was uneasy. Indeed, we may as well note at once that this story is partly the story of the relation between the "sacred" and the "secular" in the field of music, and one of the most important questions the church musician today has to ask himself is where he personally stands on that matter. This is a question which history helps us answer.

For its first three hundred years the church was technically an illicit organization within the Roman Empire. Although it was not actively persecuted all the time or in all places, church thinking was always heavily influenced by the idea that the church could not afford to involve itself with a hostile pagan world. That world disliked it and suspected it, and its values were values which the church must at many points resist.

11

That is the impression we get from all the New Testament letters—most of all, from I John. "The world," which Christians must always beware of, included the values of secular society (though it included much else as well).

Now there is not much to say about church music during the primitive period of the church—those first three hundred years. What there is to say we can leave until we come to consider the help which the Bible gives the church musician (chapter 5). But the interesting thing is this: that almost at the same time that the church became a tolerated institution (a couple of generations after that it became an official institution, the established religion of the Roman Empire) two very important things happened, one of which was the collapse of the Roman Empire itself in its old form. Look at the dates: the church was declared a tolerated religion by Constantine in A.D. 313; it was declared the official religion of the Empire by Theodosius in 380; the Roman Empire was burst wide open by the Goths in 410. The effect of this was to make it positively easier for the church to become a unifying force, at least in the west of Europe. The direction in which history began to move was, in a word, this: where the most important things were formerly said and done by the emperor in his capacity as the head of the armed forces, they were now liable to be said and done by the emperor as head of a new kind of culture. The best example is the one really well-known Roman emperor of the period after 410: Justinian (who died in 565) is known not as the conqueror of territories but as the founder of Roman law.

And most significantly, although the Goths conquered Rome, the Christians conquered the Goths. The sack of Rome did not mean a relapse into heathenism. It meant, in the end, the expansion of Christianity. There is much to be said for the view that the Christians were partly responsible for the fall of Rome; at least, some of the better Roman emperors (that is, the more responsible ones according to their standards) thought so.[4] At any rate, the missions began very soon after the collapse of the old form of Roman power.

So it became possible for Christendom suddenly to extend its boundaries, and to establish itself in Germany, in France, and in Britain, as well as in the countries around the Mediterranean. It would, of course, have remained, as it was at first, an interracial religion had it not been for the devastating consequences of the rise of Islam (or Mohammedanism), which swept over all the countries south of the Mediterranean, right up through Palestine (enveloping Jerusalem itself), and round into Turkey and the Balkans. But in Greece and South Russia the church established itself in one form—and it held its ground in the Balkans to some extent: that form was what is called the Eastern Orthodox Church, and it was separated from the Western church in 1054 and has been ever since. In the form with which we are more familiar, it established itself in the Western countries.

But—here is the second important thing that happened at that fateful time, the fourth century—the *form* in which the church established itself was dictated by a movement which had been growing up even before the church was released from its illicit status. This is the monastic movement. It may surprise modern church musicians to learn that this is just about the most important single thing that ever happened to the church and to their own status in it.

Without going into details that will not interest musicians at the moment, this is the point: that when the church began to expand, it expanded through the establishment all over Europe of centers of highly specialized religion from which religion was propagated through the surrounding area. A monastery in the most primitive days (say, the fourth century) was anything from a hermitage in which one man lived a solitary life to a considerable community in which men lived together for the single purpose of pursuing religion, supporting themselves, living by strict rules, and being committed to the achievement of a higher grade of religious life than was supposed to be possible for people who were doing the world's ordinary work.

Monasteries

This began in Africa and the Near East (actually, it can be traced to even earlier movements which were usually eccentric and even heretical or anti-social), but it formed the pattern by which Christian institutions expanded; so by the eighth century, after many shifts and surges of history, Christianity in Europe was organized through a network of religious communities staffed by dedicated people whose business was full-time religious work. In France these became

13

great institutions with hundreds of inhabitants; in Wales they were usually tiny groups.[5] In England the older cathedrals were normally the central worship places of communities of this sort.

This specialism in religion gave the opportunity for the pursuit of learning and the development of high-grade intellectual skills. The European universities themselves are an end product of the monastic system. When one remembers that at the University of Oxford it was not until 1870 that teaching members (known as "dons") were permitted either to marry or to be anything but clergy of the Church of England, one is reminded how, under this medieval system, all learning and literacy was concentrated in the church.

On another plane the distinction between the "clerk" (or "cleric": that is, the man who could write) and the "layman" is similarly marked. Inevitably, the staff of the monastery became the people who pursued religion at a professional level; religion elsewhere was "amateur." In other words, the boundary between the sacred and the secular was the monastery wall. It is hardly unfair to say that in a European medieval town religion was a matter which was left to the "clerics" to take charge of. You had prayers to say: you sent them to the monastery to be said much as you send clothes to the Chinese laundry to be washed. They were the people who could do that sort of thing better than you could.

Within the large monastery—the kind of community (often called an "abbey" with an "abbot" as its head) of which our great European cathedrals are the surviving evidences—there would be a large staff of people doing many different religious things: some at prayer, some writing books, some sweeping the cloisters, some keeping the accounts; all would meet for worship in the central place of worship, which was large enough not only to accommodate the entire staff, but to accommodate also, on Sundays and high days, the whole town if it wanted to come. The monastic staff had their places of honor at the east end of the great church, with seats; the common people stood packed in the "nave," the much larger space to the west. And as they stood they were reminded of their faith by the pictures provided by the stained-glass windows. They would be able neither to read nor to write. All specialized work was directed from the monastery.

14

What then was the church musician's place? In the first place, the only musician who could *write* would be a monk—a clerk or cleric. This gave the church musician a clear initial advantage over the secular musician, who would play and sing by ear for popular entertainment. In the second place, what the church musician sang or directed others to sing was almost entirely laid down by church tradition. In a time when everything written must be individually copied because there was no technique of printing, therefore of producing written matter in mass, any kind of change came slowly. Historians of church music can point to a considerable development of church music from the sixth century, say, to the thirteenth, but it is deceptively easy to overlook the fact that that period means seven hundred years—twenty generations.

What comes out of this is the historical fact that for a very long time indeed it was the settled and accepted condition of things that church music was entirely separated from secular music, that it was administered by professional churchmen, and that it kept itself to itself, developing very slowly, changing almost imperceptibly, subject only to local variations on traditional patterns.

Early Sacred Music

For a long time it was sung by nobody but the monastery choir and sung in unison. The words to which it was sung were for a long time completely static; they were the words of the liturgical formulae of Catholic devotion, the psalms, and a few hymns which were part of the liturgy. The sense of overall traditional discipline was high.

This, then, is the situation in the Middle Ages, the only important modifications to which we shall mention briefly in a moment:

1. Church music is the only written music.
2. It is administered and performed by professional churchmen.
3. It is the only field in which any kind of conscious musical development can be systematized when the time for that comes.
4. It is very firmly sacred and not secular.

In practice the briefest examination of any piece of plainsong music—plainsong is what the unmetrical, melodic music of

15

h is generically called—shows how differ-
metrical, dance-like music which is of

nder 3 just above that when the time
ient in music, it is in the church that we
...........bering that these are very broad generaliza-
tions which have to be modified in all sorts of details if one
wants to take the study deeper, this remains true even
when, with the spread of secular culture and philosophy
from the twelfth century onward (a result of the founding
of universities and the revival of pre-Christian classical
learning), the learned musicians of the church try their
hands at writing secular music. The one important development in music that concerns us here is, of course, the
development of *counterpoint.*

This means simply two voices singing different melodies
at the same time. Counterpoint and harmony are aspects of
the same thing: you call it harmony when you are thinking
of the sound made at any given moment by different notes
(fragments of melody) sung together; you call it counterpoint when you are thinking of the sound made by two
simultaneous systems of melody. Apparently the origin of
this was in the recognition of the elementary physical fact
that not all men's voices are comfortable within the same
pitch range. It seems to have been in the tenth century that
the custom arose of singing melodies parallel at different
pitches. Broadly speaking, it was found that the two kinds
of male voice move within compasses about a fifth apart:
the tenors would sing the melody at a certain pitch, and the
basses the same melody a fifth below.

This would have seemed a tolerable accommodation to
nature, not only because nature has provided these two
kinds of vocal equipment in human beings but also because
the fifth is, next to the octave, the most elementary, or the
most "restful" of musical intervals. (This has a physical
background: in the scheme of "harmonics," the octave is the
first harmonic of any given note; the fifth above that is the
second. To put it another way: if an organ pipe of length
x sounds the note y, then a pipe of length half-x sounds
the note an octave above y, and the pipe of length one-third
x (the next simplest fraction) sounds a note an octave-and-a-
fifth above y).

The sound made by voices singing in bare parallel fifths is to modern ears a curious sound, but in the tenth century it was a mighty discovery. It was some time before the next discovery was made, and, when it was made, it produced a revolution. You have at this stage nothing but the sacred melody being sung in parallel fifths. By what stages did church musicians reach the point at which they permitted the sacred melody to be sung accompanied by another quite different one?

Musical Revolution

You might broadly say that this happened when they started using their ears and allowing themselves to notice what they heard. Remember—this is a time when authority is everything: if what you heard sounded peculiar, it must be all right because authority said it was all right. You didn't object, "That sounds unmusical!" You just put up with it. You were happier that way. That was the prevailing mood of the ages of dogma. But the church musician tended, even in those days, to be an observant creature, and he could not help noticing this peculiar property of the scale in which he was brought up to sing.

Take this very elementary plainsong phrase—the opening line of the advent hymn, *Conditor alme siderum* ("Creator of the starry height"):

There is a beautiful musical phrase—part of one of the most beautiful hymn tunes ever composed, going far back into the middle ages of the Christian era. Now let us write it in parallel fifths:

It could not have unduly taxed even a medieval monkish ear to detect something anomalous happening at the chord marked with an asterisk. What happens there, as we have

17

written it, is that the voices are not a perfect fifth apart, but a diminished fifth, a harsh discord—the sound called by the medieval musicians the *diabolus*—the "devil's noise."

So there is a dilemma. If the lower voice sings in the same key as the upper voice (using the notes of the same scale) and follow it faithfully, it will produce this nasty sound—E natural against B flat in modern notation. If it is to follow the upper voice in perfect fifths throughout, it must sing a note—E flat—that is not in the scale used by the upper voice. It must indeed sing in its own key—which as we have written it appears to be the key of B flat. So you have two voices singing in different keys.

All this sounds very hair-splitting to a modern musician, who would say, "Well, if that's what you want to sing, why not sing it?"—or even, "It doesn't matter if it's ugly—the uglier the better!" But remember again that these were ages of authority, when people were always brought up to ask, "But what *ought* we to do?" The dialogue would have gone like this:

——— The lower voices are permitted to sing in parallel fifths with the upper voices.

——— But what about the *diabolus* under the fourth of the scale?

——— What is that?

——— If we interpret authority literally, we get a disagreeable musical noise, which is not what authority really wants, is it?

——— Agreed. Then you may modify one note in the scale to avoid this noise, but only that note, and only in those circumstances.

So what they had no doubt been doing all the time became accepted practice, and you will find in old plainsong the occasional use of the flattened seventh of the scale and the sharpened seventh in the same piece. The sign used to indicate when the note was to be flattened was a sign like a small "b," because all plainsong was noted as though it were in the key of C, and transposed to whatever key was convenient. The ambiguous note was therefore always "b," and that is the origin of our modern "flat" sign.

Just one more example of this shows how once the ear had become accustomed to hearing the harmonic implications of melody, this modification became normal and necessary.

Take now the last line of the very well-known plainsong tune *Veni Creator Spiritus* ("Come, Holy Ghost") in its original form:

Now very often in the old manuscripts it appears just like that, but it was commonly sung, perhaps always sung, like this:

The reason was that the ear began to hear the F (marked †) while it was singing the succeeding B (marked *), and it felt much more comfortable when the B was flattened. (That particular melodic pattern always induces singers and violinists to modify the upper note imperceptibly and naturally in modern performance of any kind of music.)

The Demand of Music

What is happening, then, is the musicians' noticing what *the music itself* is demanding—or what, given the permission to perform music at all, it seems natural to do. Music is coming alive, as it were, and putting problems and puzzles to the musician, who has to refer them to authority for solution. And authority is theological, dogmatic, moral; most of the time it has to say, "We hadn't thought of that. Solve it your own way."

That, of course, is a diagram. I shall not undertake to swear that any music director ever did seek out the local abbot and ask his permission to sing B flat, but if ever the abbot had been alert enough to notice it and asked a question, the musician would have replied along these lines.

That, anyhow, is the breakthrough. From there it is not a particularly long step to the stage where voices are singing independently, but making pleasing harmony with each other. It was discovered presumably somewhere in the thirteenth century that tunes could be devised which sounded

19

very well when sung uniformly by different voices, but with the voices entering at different points in time: in other words, canons and rounds. "Sumer is icumen in" (which by the way means "Summer is come in," not "coming in") is the famous archetype of that style. Here is no harmony except what results from several voices singing exactly the same tune at different time-intervals.

It looks as if things moved with a new swiftness after this. We know that authority suddenly reared its head and rebuked the church musicians for their bold experiments: in 1325 Pope John XXII directed that certain musical devices should be barred from the church and that plain and simple melody of the old kind was in future to be followed exclusively. This was because in their eagerness to experiment with an art which had suddenly showed itself to have several dimensions before unthought of, the musicians were losing sight of the meaning of the words and the fittingness of musical pyrotechnics in church.

(Anybody who wants to go further into this will be taken on to the next stage by reading my book, *The Church and Music*, the first few chapters; he can go on from there to books of real scholarship if he is so minded.)

Not to make too long a story of this, we may merely note that the stage was now set for the flowering of *polyphonic* music (music for many voices in many parts), which by the sixteenth century reached its greatest heights of achievement in the hands of Tallis, Palestrina, Lassus, and Byrd. The normal form of church music throughout this period was the *cantus firmus*—a plainsong or traditional tune—decorated by the addition of several other vocal parts. The *cantus firmus* was, or was supposed to be, well known to the listener, and it was sung by the *tenor* (so called because he "held"—*tenere*—the whole thing together by singing the familiar tune). Below him was the *bassus* —which simply means the low voice. Above him would be the *altus*—the high voice (high, that is, in relation to the tenor). This might be sufficient; music in this form—and in forms with any of the voices divided into two or more parts—could all be sung by grown men, the *altus* singing as what we now call a male alto or countertenor. If you brought in the boys from the choir school, which certainly was part of the "campus" in a large monastic foundation,

then you could get one or two parts called *soprano*
—meaning simply "on top," and you would have your
full four- or five-part choir, all hung round the well-known
tune that the tenor sang, which linked the new composition
with the old tradition. It was only at the late stages that
specially composed pieces were admitted to the church
—pieces, that is, in which no well-known tune found a
place. But the whole process developed to a lofty degree of
sophistication, as can be seen if you look at the magnificent
antiphonal music in ten or twelve parts written for Mark's
Venice by Gabrieli, or at the monumental *Spem in alium
nunquam habui* ("My hope has never been in any other
but thee") composed by Thomas Tallis in the mid-sixteenth
century in forty real parts (eight five-part choirs).[6]

Eve of Reformation

By the time the Reformation took place, then, church music
is in the following position. It has become a highly developed
and subtle medium of expression, still wholly under the
charge of the church, still widely separated from secular
music, still performed by choirs which are the lineal descendants of the monks' choirs in the old abbeys and monasteries,
still associated primarily with the liturgical words which are
part of the Catholic church's complex scheme of worship.
Choirs are employed not to lead congregational singing but
to sing music to which the congregation merely listens—to
sing, in fact, the whole of the service, in antiphony with
the clergy appointed to sing or say the parts of the service
allotted to the priest. The question whether a church
musician shall or shall not continue to be primarily a cleric
and only secondarily a musician is on the point of breaking
out into the open. The assumption is that he will be a
cleric. But since (a) music has become so highly sophisticated an art already as to demand a full-time autonomous
artist for its practice, and (b) there is by now so much
interplay between sacred and secular music, whatever the
official administrative mind of the church may think, the
tension between the demands of theology and those of music
in its own right is mounting to the breaking point. Taverner,
one of the greatest of the English contemporaries of Tallis,
composed a Mass which is nowadays well known—called
"Westron Wynde"; the implication of the title is that a

21

secular tune of that name plays a leading part in its structure. During the later Middle Ages the carol had arisen to bridge the gap between sacred and secular: words of a semi-secular kind were associated with the doctrines of the faith and sung to secular ballad tunes. And to add to all this, schismatic sects, the precursors of organized Protestantism, were singing songs of their own—religious songs of great evangelical intensity—to tunes of the secular, dance-like kind. The old assumptions about the church musician are going to come under heavy fire, and some of them are going to disappear for good. The secret of this historically is that the Reformation itself was a product of the same forces which produced also the great outbreak of art and philosophy at the end of the Middle Ages. It is no coincidence that the founders of modern Protestantism came on the scene just when church music had fully "found itself."

2
Professional or Amateur?

The New Question

The Reformation brought out into the open the question of whether the church musician should be a professional or an amateur, and there it has remained ever since.

For our purposes here it is necessary only to distinguish between the Reformation according to Luther and the Reformation according to Calvin. But perhaps it is even more important to remember that at what we call the Reformation (which after all was not a single event but a very diverse complex of events) not everything in the life of the church was changed all at once. Indeed, Luther and Calvin are often judged as though they hoped to sweep away every medieval doctrine and custom that existed in their own youth. This is a mistake.

Luther the Artist

From the musician's point of view the important thing about Luther was that he was a musician; he was, indeed, an artist in many fields, not least in the art of rhetoric. Our own hymnals are evidence that he both composed music and wrote lyrics.[7] His attitude to the church's worship was, compared with all the other reformers, remarkably conservative. There was much about the traditional Mass that he loved—not least its music. He wanted to keep a great deal of it unaltered. He had to be persuaded even to turn it into German for his own congregations. Whatever Luther did achieve as a reformer he achieved as the consequence of one settled conviction. This conviction was that traditional church institutions were standing between man and his personal encounter with God. His doctrine of "justification by faith alone" is a statement of the belief that God's forgiveness is personally available for the believer and need not be applied for through church officials or paid for by church dues and taxes. He wanted his churchmanship and worship to express that. What needed to be altered in order to get that said he altered, but much else he would have left unchanged had it not been for the more radical opinions of his associates.

The involved politics of the Lutheran Reformation do not concern us here, nor do the details of Luther's teaching. What does concern us is that, as all the reformers after him, Luther saw in music a chance to symbolize in worship the believer's direct access to God. He was not content that the worshiper should watch worship being professionally conducted on his behalf. He wanted the worshiper's belief objectified and sustained by proper preaching (which the medieval church had forgotten how to do), and he wanted the believer to sing.

Hence the Lutheran hymn—that which is often called the "chorale." The typical Lutheran hymn is a lyric set to a tune founded as often as not on a secular melody which everybody could easily sing together. Now the real Lutheran chorales, those of the 1524 vintage, usually sound strange to modern ears. We know "A mighty fortress is our God" well enough, but we very rarely sing it as it was sung when it first appeared. The rhythm of these tunes is all-important; it is vivid, syncopated, and exceedingly singable when you are used to it, but it sounds strange to people who are used to regular bars, as most of us are. This must not make any of us think that the Lutheran tune was a highbrow, specialized, arty kind of music. Nowadays it almost sounds like that when people try to perform it. But in those days it connected directly with popular music, carol music, troubadour music. It was just what people were used to singing outside church. Goodness knows who it really was who said, "Why should the devil have all the good tunes?" Some attribute that to General Booth, some to Wesley, some to Luther. Luther, anyhow, could have said it, because as those other two song-evangelists, he made it his business to cross the forbidden frontier between sacred and secular music. Let it be music, he said, we will make it as sacred as it need be.

Calvin the Disciplinarian

When we come to John Calvin of Geneva, we are in a different climate altogether. In common with Luther he held that man must be released from his bondage to institutions and told that the promises of God were available to him personally. But Calvin was not an artist. Where Luther saw things in terms of images, Calvin saw them in terms of concepts. He wrote a system of Christian doctrine which was a reinterpretation of traditional doctrine, stripping away the accretions of custom and going back to the Bible and the earliest Christian authorities. He was in doctrine, you might say, an ultraconservative. The popular notion of Calvin as a flinty-hearted dogmatist who consigned most of the world to hell and said that this was God's will is a caricature based on a few pages in a late edition of his *Institutes of the Christian Religion*. But where Luther was a buoyant explorer of religion and politics, Calvin was a tortured disciplinarian in his methods; where Luther wanted a flowering of local religion hand in hand with a new enlightened nationalism (Luther's Bible is, it may be remembered, the very fountain-head of the modern German language), Calvin wanted a true theocracy in Geneva, and the outward emphasis in his church from 1541 to his death in 1564 was on discipline. When the citizens transgressed the law, the elders of the church, who were also the magistrates, should deal with him.

Now this meant an attitude to professionalism in music very different from that of Luther. Luther would have welcomed a choir to sing some of the service if the people were allowed to sing a substantial part of it; he could have done without the choir, but not without congregational song. But he did not absolutely forbid choirs; Calvin did. Calvin ruled that there should be no music whatever in public worship except what could be sung by all present, and this must be sung in unison without any kind of instrumental accompaniment. He was not the first to talk in this way, but he was the first to do it influentially. Moreover, nothing must be sung which was not literally based on the Bible, and this means no hymns—only metrical psalms.

It was a merciful accident that brought him into touch with one of the best folk-artists of the time, Louis Bourgeois, and with a court poet, Clément Marot, who had begun to make elegant translations of the psalms into meter for the amusement of the French court. Calvin caused a metrical psalter to be prepared, based on the pattern of Marot's poetry, and set Bourgeois to provide music for it. What emerged was some very delightful poetry—far, far more lyrical and beautiful than the English metrical psalms of the same period—and some of the greatest congregational music that has ever graced the pages of Christian music. Bourgeois again went to secular sources for some of his tunes, but he did not model them on the troubadour music that Luther took for his models, because the words he was required to set were in meters that the old folk music would hardly fit. So he adapted the tunes, or composed them, and you have only to look at the style of the French Psalters as exemplified in the first Genevan Psalm (first printed in this form in 1542) to see what a magnificent "congregational sense" Bourgeois had. Look at this tune of Psalm 1 and observe its judicious use of repetition, its beautifully placed climax, and its sense of melodic development, all of which make it, despite its great length, so easy to memorize:

The tune we call the *Old 100th* is the best-known tune from this source, but so many of the others are wonderful music that it is a pity that so few of them are known to modern congregations.

The Difference

It may be a pity, but it is, like so many things that move one to that kind of protest, a clue to history. Watch it closely. Calvin was exceedingly restrictive in his use of church music.

So much so that when Bourgeois wanted to publish a harmonized edition of some of his psalm tunes, this had to be published not in Switzerland but in France, and in the end (some time after 1551) Bourgeois resigned with his work half done after a dispute with Calvin on this very subject. Calvin was then the archenemy of professional church music. The only thing for a church musician to do in his dispensation was provide folk songs for everybody to sing, and, presumably, act as a song leader in public worship. There was no organ for him to play, and no choir for him to train or to write anthems for.

But here is a curious paradox that church musicians might well ponder. The facts are that in the common folk song of western Protestants, far more of the Lutheran hymnody is known than of Calvin's hymnody. I do not mean here to take account of Lutheran tunes that only Lutherans know, or of Genevan psalms that only strict Calvinists know. I refer rather to the "export value" of the two different kinds of music. The Lutheran chorale continued to propagate itself with great flexibility and success right down to 1715. The Genevan psalm stopped dead at 1562, when the 150 psalms with their music were finally published.

Think for a moment how many great Lutheran tunes are among the best-known hymns. I suppose that the list would be more or less this:

Nun danket (Now thank we all our God) -	1647
Lobe den Herren (Praise to the Lord) -	1665
Ein' feste Burg (A mighty fortress) -	1529
Unser Herrscher (See the morning sun) -	1680
Christus, der ist mein Leben (O Lord, our Lord) -	1609
Herzlich tut mich Verlangen (O sacred head) -	1613
Valet will ich dir geben (All glory, laud, and honour) -	1613
Nun freut euch (We come unto our fathers' God) -	1524

—well, need we go further? Consult your index of sources and see how fruitfully the Lutheran strain has enriched universal hymnody. Contrast the Genevan contribution. It consists, if one is to take the broad view of the *Old 100th* and the *Old 124th*. Many other Genevan tunes are well known to experts in church music; quite a number appear in the hymnals. But they are not among those tunes which you can ever be sure that a congregation will know.

This is not a criticism. It is history. What it tells us is that

Calvin's rigid fundamentalism produced a small quantity of church music of the very highest quality which proved to be of strictly local usefulness. The secret of this was his insistence on metrical psalms. No new hymns could be written, so no new tunes were wanted. What they had were magnificent, but hardly anybody else has ever found a use for them. Let me repeat—there is music here which anybody would be the better for learning. I merely record that hardly anybody has actually done so, whereas the Lutheran tunes have invaded all Protestant hymnody to stay.[8]

The paradoxical thing is this: that in his zeal for the suppression of musical professionalism (the music of the few) and the liberation of musical amateurism (the music of the many), Calvin produced what has turned out to be the music of a few after all. He has left us with a body of hymnody which the highly literate know and rejoice in, but which has not become *folk* hymnody. It's only the professionals who really know the Genevan psalm tunes. Somewhere along the line the project of liberating music collapsed in Calvin's case. Too much insistence on the doctrine that the only professionals in church are clergy and elders stifles *popular* music as well as professional music. One gets the feeling that Calvin at Geneva was so overanxious to protect his people from religious professionalism that would stand between them and God that he overreached himself; he became rather like the mother who took her family to the seaside for a treat and was heard saying furiously to her young son, "I brought you here to enjoy yourself, and enjoy yourself *you will.*"

Vox Populi

It was the English and Scottish who found a compromise. The English Reformation was already well on its course when Calvin's psalters were being published, and an English metrical psalter, incomplete but historic, was published in 1549; the complete version was published in 1562. Between those two dates came the short reign of Queen Mary (1553-58), during which Protestant leaders were in serious jeopardy and fled to the continent of Europe. Those who went to Geneva encountered the Genevan psalmody in its full glory. At something of a loss to find tunes for their own 1549 metrical psalter, they said at Geneva, *"This* is exactly what we were looking for." But the Genevan tunes could not be exported as they stood, for nearly all of them were in meters entirely foreign to the English manner. For, whereas there were more than a hundred different meters in the Genevan psalter when it was finished, the English psalter confined itself to a very few. Virtually all the psalms were translated in the same meter—what we call "Common Meter"—the variations could be counted on the fingers of two hands. So when the English exiles returned, inspired though they were with the Genevan form of psalm tune, their task was to write tunes on the Genevan model but in the English meter.

The history of hymn-singing during the next century in England has a rude humanity which we do not find in Geneva. For, whereas the enthusiasts who returned from Switzerland naturally wanted to preserve as much of the Genevan style as they could, and indeed tried sometimes to rewrite the English metrical psalms so that the great Genevan tunes would fit them without too much alteration, popular opinion speedily curbed their enthusiasm. The fact was that a tune such as Psalm 1, which we quoted above, proved to be simply too long and demanding for the rustic and not naturally musical Englishman. (Not that there is any evidence that he even tried to sing that one, but others as beautiful and as exacting were tried and were soon rejected.) He found he preferred a tune in the old ballad meter of his own metrical psalms, and at that, he preferred it to run half the length that the oldest tunes even of the English kind ran. The ideal had certainly been to provide one tune for each of the 150 psalms—each to have what was called its "proper" tune. A number of these old tunes, dating from 1558 onward, still survive in hymnals, though they are not much sung congregationally even now, but when you see a tune name in the form "Old 30th" or "Old 136th," that name signifies that it was designed in the mid-sixteenth century for that psalm and for no other.

But the system broke down because the congregations would not have it. And what the congregation preferred was more highly respected by the English song leaders than it was by John Calvin. Calvin would have said, "What do their preferences matter?" The English precentor was more likely to say, "If they won't, they won't." So the tunes that really gained popularity—and that continue to appear in hymnal after hymnal right from their inception to the present day—turned out to be tunes of two lines, whereas the original "Anglo-Genevan" tunes were of four lines. (I am sorry to be pedantic, but that is the proper way to look at them musically. A line means fourteen syllables; a verse of "O God, Our Help in Ages Past" is, on the scale I am using, a verse of two lines.) These tunes were short, easily remembered, and were suitable to any psalm. They are not called "Old *x*th"; they have names such as "French," "Windsor," "Dunfermline," "Winchester Old," and "York."

Now not to weary the reader with historical *minutiae*, let me simply make this point: it was these anonymous, simple, sturdy, splendid tunes which really "caught on." Genevan hymnody became, as it were, "set solid." Here was your psalter, 150 psalms each with its "proper" tune. So there was never any need for any new tunes; you sang either the proper tune or no tune. But in England a new principle arose. Not only were the new short tunes easy to learn, but, if you could write one new tune to Psalm 23, why could you not write another?

A study of English hymnody up to about 1660 shows the fascinating picture of professionalism versus amateurism. The leading musicians constantly wanted people either to go back to the great tunes of Geneva or to learn new tunes which reflected the Genevan style, but popular opinion continued to prefer the "common" tunes. They are, as anybody who ever goes to church knows, magnificent examples of simple music. They wear like leather. They show a perfection not only of outward form but of popular sympathy unrivalled anywhere except in the traditional carols of Christendom. These were not days in which popular opinion sought the basest in music; they were, relatively, days of innocence. Just one example will make any further argument unnecessary:

This tune first appeared in print in 1592; very likely it had been in common use for up to thirty years before that. Most of its phrases appear in a longer tune, dating from forty years earlier, by Christopher Tye.[9] But amateur music has no conscience about copyright. Nobody will ever know who composed it. Possibly somebody improvised it, having some knowledge of the earlier tune. It does not matter. The point is that it is pure "natural music," with a sense of climax (hinted at by the asterisk in our example) that comes direct from Geneva.

It is the special historic excellence of that age that popular taste centered on what has become recognized as fine music, though it was simple music. The main reason for this was not any special virtue in the Englishman of 1600, but rather the very simple fact that there was not nearly so much music to choose from, and not nearly so wide a musical vocabulary available to the ordinary man. The more he came to know, the more liable he was to choose the poorer in preference to the better. In that age it was still possible to choose the simpler in preference to the more difficult without floundering in bad music.

But the professionals never gave up hope. There were the fine musicians of the time—Thomas Tallis in the years around 1560, Orlando Gibbons sixty years later, Henry Lawes twenty years later still, all of whom wrote psalm tunes for private publications which were never sung in public in those days, although all three are found in our hymnals nowadays—much to our benefit. Then there were pedagogic church musicians such as the editors of the 1635 Scottish Psalter. This was a capital example of professional failure to communicate. Scotland had produced a music edition of its own metrical psalms in 1564. In 1635 certain people thought a new edition was called for, and a very fine book was indeed published, with a few new tunes and a number of Genevan tunes restored to their "proper" psalms. But it never caught the congregational imagination. It remains a museum piece. It was a gesture toward the raising of musical standards and the widening of musical taste that simply failed to get a response.[10]

All this shows us how it was possible in a certain kind of post-Reformation society for the popular, amateur taste in music to take control quite firmly, and to resist the pressures of the professional musician. These common tunes became the folk song of both Anglican and Puritan congregations. Only metrical psalms were permitted in either kind of church; the most popular tunes to them were these fine, simple unison melodies.

But note this: these melodies were very definitely *church music*. You have only to look at any contemporary carol tune, or secular tune, to see how far the psalm tunes were from the secular idiom. (See, for example, "God rest you merry," or "What child is this?".) There is virtually nothing in common between the familiar psalm tune and the equally familiar carol or secular tune; the psalm tune is always more staid, more serene, less energetic, and above all less dance-like than the secular tune. The Lutherans of the same period were capable of much greater approximations to secular styles than the English psalm-singers were.

What we seem to have, then, in the days of the foundation of the hymn tune, is a society which is firmly walled around by sacred discipline; it is a separated society, but it manages to become, in Britain, a *folk*. The psalms with their tunes become almost national songs—they certainly became in the fullest sense national songs in Scotland. There was a genius here which could at the same time accept the underlying authority of Geneva and Calvinism, and yet could create new things within that authority—devise new tunes which were at once taken up as popular religious songs. To this extent the church musician was an unknown person; he was not an instrumentalist but a song leader, and it was he who selected, and certainly sometimes invented, these popular tunes. He often adapted them from sources he knew (as happened with "Winchester Old" quoted above). No matter where it came from, in his hands it became a kind of song which bound the Christian folk together and separated it from "the world." This happened to be exactly what *that* Christian *folk* wanted; just as in earlier days the Christian *folk* loved its semi-secular carols and its free intercourse with the world.

After the deaths of William Byrd (d. 1623) and Orlando Gibbons (d. 1625) there were no really great professional church musicians for a long generation. Church song gained all the impetus it needed from the popular psalm tunes, and the Puritan ascendancy of Oliver Cromwell confined music-making to the home, largely suppressing it in church.

Return to the Professional

It was the restoration of the monarchy in 1660, when King Charles II returned to the throne of England, that heralded a swing back to the professional outlook. At once the values of Calvinist Puritanism were publicly reversed. The choir of the Chapel Royal—always a very powerful influence in English professional church music—was revived, and with it many of the cathedral choirs were revived as well. Charles II sent his best court musicians to France so that they could catch up with a hundred years of musical development, and what they ran into was the first century of continental opera. This was enough to produce a radical change of fashion in both sacred and secular music. The new music was music that permitted for the first time a virtuoso technique, the eminence of a soloist, music with elaborate melody accompanied by instruments, music expressing in a new way dramatic values. The end product of this, at its best, was Purcell (1659-95), and Purcell's music is the same music whether it is written for sacred or for secular occasions. Music had taken another leap forward toward self-government, as it were. Music was now, even more than in Palestrina's time, *music;* whether it was used for secular or for sacred ends was secondary—indeed, musically the distinction was immaterial.

The effect this had on church music was principally to cause us all to begin to dance in church. That is to say, church music, which had always rather carefully avoided the discipline of regular bars and metrical accents (the psalm tunes had a primitive rhythm as expressive as that of plainsong; it was never dead regular, except, significantly, occasionally in the hands of the professionals) in the new kind of anthem and hymn tune had an absolutely regular beat. It was either a march or a minuet. Take *The Methodist Hymnal* and turn first to no. 323—one of the most perfect of the Genevan tunes; observe its irregular yet very expressive rhythm. Then turn to no. 57, "Dunfermline," and reconstitute it with long notes at the beginning of phrases 1 and 3, and as the *second* notes of phrases 2 and 4, and you have the typical primitive psalm tune rhythm. Glance at no. 56, "Irish," and see what the new music provided in the way of expressive melody and dance-like measure.

There is—this we must emphasize—a connection between the reappearance of the professional musician as a person of consequence in society (sacred or secular) and the new approach of church music toward the secular. Music is music to a musician; it is sacred or secular to an amateur. This principle will be confirmed as we go on.

The next dramatic development in church music history is the appearance of the Wesleys. Their music was, we find, unashamedly secular. That tune "Irish" which we have just looked at is one of the more sober of the early Methodist tunes. But why were the Wesleyan tunes in this sense secular? Because their composers as often as not came from the opera houses; because those who first sanctioned them knew the music of Handel and Pepusch better than any other music. Nobody can really distinguish between a sacred and a secular style in Handel. Sufficient proof of that is to be found in the universal sacred associations of the song, "Ombra mai fu," which when dressed in Sunday clothes is called "Handel's Largo." Although no English musician knew anything of J. S. Bach in the eighteenth century, exactly the same is true of Bach. "Jesu, Joy of man's desiring," from Church Cantata 147, is a wholly acceptable secular concert piece. There is nothing sacred, except the accidental associations of the organ, about any of Bach's organ preludes and fugues; what is the difference in style between the great Prelude and Fugue in G (S 541) and the admittedly "sacred" chorale prelude "In thee is joy"?

The first Wesley musicians were professional musicians —I do not mean "great composers," although Handel himself did write a little music especially for Wesleyan use; I mean men who moved in the world of music and made their living by it. The typical first-generation Wesley musician was J. F. Lampe, a bassoonist at Covent Garden. The point is not that Lampe was a composer of international stature —he was not—but that he had *The Beggar's Opera* and *Rodelinda* and *Dido and Aeneas* in his bones.

3
Sacred and Secular

The Encounter

The really important point is now emerging. What we are really talking about is "sacred" and "secular" and whether these are legitimate categories at all in the study of church music. Let us continue the story and see where it leads us.

One of the ways of looking at church music history produces the conclusion that the style oscillates between a sacred emphasis and a secular emphasis. The point to which we have just got is one when the pendulum had swung toward the secular end of the scale. It looks, moreover, as if church music periodically suffered injections of secular music, through the influence of professionals, yet between those periods it settled down into an amateur period during which it assimilated, benefited from, and then grew tolerant (in medical terms) of, the injection. Look what happened to Wesleyan music. The "vintage" Methodist tunes—such as "Irish," or many of the more complex and florid melodies of the period, say, 1742-60—are very able reflections of the grace and expressiveness of operatic melody. They are often influenced by Purcell. The later ones are influenced by Handel. But it is interesting to note that very few of the vintage Methodist tunes are in common currency now; of church anthems, most of the really fine music written in the eighteenth century by Boyce, Greene, Battishill, and their contemporaries have been the subject of fairly strenuous revival during the past generation. By contrast, what people often call "old Methodist tunes," or—save the mark!—"good old Methodist tunes" are tunes from a much later period

—usually after 1800. The history of the music of the evangelical revival, which gave John Wesley himself displeasure that he did not hesitate to express, shows the growth of the highly operatic "repeating" tune out of the much more demanding and musical "Wesley tune." Glance at no. 72 in *The Methodist Hymnal*—the tune "Diadem," which people still refer to as a (good) old Methodist tune. Look at the composer's dates—1819-99. Then look at its bass, and contrast the harmonic barrenness implied by that bass with the bass of "Irish" (no. 56).

The direction which popular church music took within the period of the first stages of the evangelical revival was toward abundant rhetoric and away from musical integrity. The index of this is simply in the comparative ratings of harmony and counterpoint in two tunes such as "Diadem" and "Irish." Both are designed to set a stanza of identical length; one accommodates the music precisely to the words, the other demands a great deal of repetition of the words. One has a well-balanced melody, weighted emotionally toward its far end as all traditional popular melodies are, using the material that secular music provided in its best manifestations. The other is melodically a string of phrases each of which is shapely in its own right but which, as a sequence, show no overall sense of melodic purpose. One has a judicious balance of bass with treble, that is, a good melody-and-bass counterpoint; the other uses a bass almost entirely confined to the keynote, the fourth, and the fifth, bringing every line to an end on a perfect cadence in the home key.

This is not an isolated example; indeed, if one looks at tunes such as "Wareham" (no. 29), "Truro" (no. 198), "St. Stephen" (no. 356), one can see the strength of the earlier "Wesleyan," post-Purcellian tunes, which ably but modestly use the new vocabulary that secular music had made available. He finds, on the other hand, a progressive tendency toward more notes and less music as the style wears itself out in the early nineteenth century.

At its best, eighteenth-century popular church music expresses the warmth and hospitality of the evangelical revival. The best of their tunes *sound* like an invitation to believe. The worst of their tunes sound like an invitation to *conform*. (You might say that at their best the old psalm tunes sound like an invitation to join an army or an expedition.) But quite undoubtedly the degeneracy into tunes with more rhetoric than sense, such as "Diadem" (which in this, by the way, is very far inferior to the rugged integrity of either of the other tunes to "All hail the power"), correspond with a movement away from the vital sources of secular music. The great tunes of that period recall the great tunes of contemporary opera. The poor tunes of a later period develop a style which is much less easily paralleled in secular music. They become in a way "churchy." But it is a different kind of churchiness from that of the psalm tunes. It is a churchiness that derives from a neglect of the world, not from a theological defiance of the world. This is vitally important. Musically it amounts to this: that "Irish" is a fine tune not least because it stems from a school of composition led by people such as the professional Lampe who moved among music in their secular life. They were able to handle the greatly increased complexity of musical expression, and to use the new instruments of expressiveness judiciously. "Diadem" was written by a song leader who spent his working life in a hat factory, and who in his style imitated the older church music, deriving nothing from what was really going on in music when he was composing.

It really seems, then, as if the professional is going to become more and more important in church music as music becomes more complex. This is going to prove to be true; but the gulf between the professional and the amateur is for the same reason going to widen rather than become narrower. The problem, which succeeding ages will all be equally shy of facing, is going to become more acute the longer they wait. We have 150 more years of history yet to cover, and these will show us how alarmingly the rate of growth of that problem accelerates.

The Heyday of Amateur Music

The nineteenth century in Britain and in Europe generally is the heyday of church music amateurism and of the "church style." The church musician's place became more conspicuous, but no less ambiguous, during that time.

The early years of that century saw a major revolution in music-making whose chief cause was the founding in 1811 of the house of Novello. Novello was the first to perfect the technique of cheap music printing. Not much later came the wave of "singing classes" especially associated with the large industrial towns of England, and with the names of such song leaders as Hullah, Mainzer, and Curwen the publisher, who invented the so-fa system of notation to help singers with easy sight-singing. A huge demand for simple music grew up even before the coming of universal education in 1870 produced the school demand with which we are now very familiar. Many such song-schools grew up around large churches, especially non-Anglican churches, and choral societies flourished into great prosperity.

Along with this came the developments within the church: the Oxford movement (from 1833 onward) which caused the Church of England to overhaul the whole of its worship program and which, when its energies were directed to the point by S. S. Wesley, promoted the more serious pursuit of church music; the great growth of large non-Anglican churches in the industrial centers, with considerable choirs growing out of the song-schools and choral societies; and, from about 1870 onward, the second evangelical awakening associated with the names of General Booth of the Salvation Army (1865) and of the American evangelists Moody and Sankey. In amongst all this we must note the obscure but significant fact that the use of hymns in the Church of England was legalized in 1821. (Many evangelically minded Anglican churches had been singing hymns long before this, but it was possible to object to it on legal grounds; it was such an objection which led to a test case, as a result of which hymns were explicitly permitted.) The demand for Anglican hymnals to illustrate specifically Anglican worship, rather than hymnals of the dissenting kind which were manuals of teaching and devotion, produced a great deal of activity on the part of editors.

Status and Its Problems

One can see how the status of the church musician was bound to rise in such conditions. And we have noted what was the origin of the appearance of choirs in non-Anglican churches. It will be remembered that the choir in the Anglican church was always a traditional part of its appointment, even though under Puritan opinion the choir virtually disappeared from the ordinary parish church, and when it was revived in the eighteenth century its place was in a choir loft at the back of the church, and the accompaniment was provided often by a band of local musicians playing conventional orchestral instruments. But church music in the Anglican church as a whole in the early nineteenth century was very ill-appointed, and the provision of a full-sized organ in such a church was almost unheard of. Popular music in the nonconformist churches was far more prosperous and strenuous. The Oxford movement moved the choir to the front of the church again, reviving in this as in much else the customs of the Middle Ages. This made the musicians more visually conspicuous, and a large change of emphasis in church music was the inevitable result. Given a better standing for the choir director and a better endowment for the choir, the next requirement was music for the choir to sing, and the onsurge of music in churches of this kind was choral rather than congregational. One notes that in hymnals of the time hymn tunes are printed in keys which do not presuppose unison congregational singing and are composed in styles which are clearly derived from the part song, not the popular carol or unison song. It was the promotion of choirs that was responsible for this.

But for all that, the choir in the Anglican church had an ancient origin. What we have to notice is that the choir in the Puritan church has no ancient origin. A Congregational church in 1860, for example, if it were in a populous area, would be built with a large provision for the choir and would be provided with a choir of forty or fifty voices. Older churches were built with no such provision, and were content with congregational singing. And there is no provision for a choir—a semi-professional musical body, that is—in the principles on which the Congregational, Baptist, and Presbyterian churches were founded in Britain and in Europe. It was a purely social movement, we are bound to say a purely secular movement, that provided non-Anglican churches with choirs in the nineteenth century. There was nothing theological or liturgical about it, as there was about the origin of the Anglican choir.

Quick Results

The degeneration in the quality and inflation of the quantity of church music in the nineteenth century is familiar enough not to require detailed account here. What it is worthwhile to remember is that this degeneration and inflation are to be found in all music of that period. The revolution in English and European society has a good deal to do with it. Cheap labor, cheap products, and cheap industrial values are reflected faithfully in a great outpouring of cheap music for solo singers, choirs, and pianists. Cheap music has never had much of a run in the concert hall simply because at the production level music for a large orchestra cannot be cheap, but at the domestic level cheap music had a ready sale.

The romantic movement in music had added yet another dimension of expressiveness and relaxed yet more conventions. In the eighteenth century musical "form" is almost a dogma; form governs content, and the expression of intimate and profound issues in music requires the genius of a Haydn or a Mozart. The great bulk of eighteenth-century music is, like eighteenth-century architecture, urbane, reserved, and ceremonious, not exploring the depths of human experience or emotion. From Beethoven onward there is an enormous amount that music is permitted to do and say that occurred only to the highest geniuses of the eighteenth century; it becomes true that with far less discipline and effort it is possible to produce highly evocative musical effects, so that correspondingly a new kind of genius is required to keep all the new resources in order. That genius is displayed by Beethoven (but what you really want to do is study Beethoven's music down to the posthumous quartets, and see how much of the earlier exuberance he renounced in his later work). It is displayed by Schubert, Berlioz, Chopin, Brahms, and Wagner. But the vocabulary which these could use with such precise and telling effect could equally be used by hacks and showmen; when they used it, the results were much more disastrous than when hacks wrote in the eighteenth-century style.

And since it happened that at this time Western religion entered a highly emotional and individualistic phase, what the church most welcomed was highly emotional music —music that used this new vocabulary as carelessly as a pretentious journalist uses the vocabulary of psychology. Too often it hardly mattered what the content was, so long as the outward form was highly colored, emotionally restless, and full of emphatic ornament. Victorian music, in fact, is just like Victorian domestic architecture—all spikes and turrets and emphatic gestures, no matter how trifling its content.

The question is, what was the relation between this and secular music? Was there really a "church style" in the Victorian era? I am inclined to think that there was, and that it was produced by something not quite like the forces that had produced the church style either of the Puritan psalms or of the early nineteenth-century evangelistic music.

There is no doubt that secular influences in, say, the church music of 1860-90 were very well marked. I sometimes refer to the striking manner in which the most telling phrase in Liszt's *Liebesträume* appears in several hymn tunes of this period; the most notable of these quotations is in an exuberantly sentimental tune of Barnby preserved in *The Methodist Hymnal,* no. 169. "Just as I am":

But there is a close affinity between the Victorian hymn tune and the Victorian domestic ballad. Barnby's "When morning gilds the skies" (properly interpreted, not as bad a tune as most that he wrote) is schematically the same as his ballad "Sweet and Low." The familiar tune to "Dear Lord and Father of mankind" could equally be an intimate love song by any third-rate drawing-room composer of the time. And that egregious pomposity, "National Hymn" (no. 552), would have done very well for a large-scale chorus in an opera by Offenbach. In the continental Catholic church there was virtually a sell-out to the operatic style in the Masses and occasional pieces written by composers of the school of Gounod.

The new thing about the nineteenth century, as we said, was that there was now so much music about. More and more it was, in the secular field, invading the lives of ordinary people. So the church musician, although he might be an amateur, or a professional only within the church field, could not be ignorant of what was happening in music at large. The Anglican and nonconformist musicians consciously or unconsciously used the part songs and ballads as their models; the new evangelists used the music-hall songs. But what distinguishes the church style which undoubtedly did develop in the hands of people such as Barnby, Stainer, J. B. Dykes, and Goss, is the *selection* they made, again consciously or unconsciously, from the available music of the secular world.[11]

Secular music was plumbing the greatest depths in chamber music and symphonic music. Perhaps only Verdi and Wagner, each in his different way, were solving the special problem of handling all the resources which the new music made available for opera. But music at its indisputably greatest was the music of metaphysic, the music of questing freethinkers, music divorced from religious or social dogma. And it was attracting an almost religious attention on the part of listeners. It was not now, as so much of Mozart's and Haydn's historically was, written for the amusement of the affluent. It was written to share profundities with a much wider listening group. Mozart and Haydn were listened to in a manner in which they were never listened to in their lifetimes. The rapidly increasing musical public was preparing the way for the twentieth-century phenomenon of music for the masses (symbolically represented in Henry Wood's foundation of the Promenade Concerts in 1895).

Romantic Excesses

But religion was never less metaphysical, never more romantically sensational, in Europe than it was in the nineteenth century. It does not matter where you touch it, the answer is the same. In English nonconformity and in the Church of Scotland—the Calvinist traditions—the artist-preacher was at his height. He might or might not base himself in classic Christian doctrine (in Scotland he normally did, in England he normally did not); it was rhetoric which counted, and which people queued to hear in the great churches. Corresponding with this was the romantic pursuit of ancient liturgies and ancient music, the revival of picturesque medieval customs, and the building of cathedral-like neo-Gothic church buildings in Anglicanism under the Oxford movement. Similarly corresponding was the cult of highly emotional music and popular pageantry in continental Catholic churches. The same historical movement that brought metaphysical music to its maturity, giving it in

Beethoven's hands an impetus that drove it clean through the trivia of romanticism to the bedrock of reason and the very fountainheads of emotion, attacked religion and pried it away from dogma and discipline. Popular religion, therefore, really could not use Beethoven. The "great" composers of the nineteenth century hardly wrote for the church, and anyhow (if you omit the debatable exception of Beethoven's *Missa Solemnis*) never wrote at their best for it. There was nothing in Schubert's G major String Quartet or in the Fourth Symphony of Brahms that was any use whatever to popular religion.

So the musicians of the church simply skimmed off the surface of the music. To the ordinary churchman Beethoven and Schubert were composers of occasionally attractive tunes, and Chopin was the composer of the *Nocturne in E flat*. The "tunes" and the harmonies in which these composers dealt on a grand scale were pressed into service to kindle and keep alive religious emotion. But the qualities that made great music great in those days were different from the corresponding qualities in the previous century. Earlier, a decorous melody and modest harmony within a conventional musical form went most of the way; now it was the building of long paragraphs of music, the working out of subtle musical arguments, the large scenes and long perspectives which counted more. Further, the great music of the time was largely instrumental, rather than vocal. (Who, with the most unscrupulous talent for lifting good tunes from the classics, could make a hymn tune out of the opening of Beethoven's *Appassionata?*) This basic fact, that argument and reason undergird the emotional and expressive surface of romantic music, ignored even now by the careless music-lover, was at least admitted then to make this kind of music essentially unfitted for popular use. Hence, of course, a new distinction between "popular" and "classical" music. But hence also the process by which church musicians, hoping to express subjective religion, made use of the surface qualities but not of the heart of classical music for their purposes.

I fancy that this is the secret of the unsatisfactoriness of much nineteenth-century church music, and we may nowadays take warning from it. The "church style" proved to be the secular romantic style *minus* reason and responsi-

43

bility. Now there is a great deal of very good nineteenth-century church music: some of S. S. Wesley's anthems, for example, or hymn tunes such as "Regent Square," "Lauda anima," and "St. Gertrude" have a genuine character and strength that is peculiarly of this period. The nineteenth century in Europe was, after all, an age of confidence and progress and of optimism (it may have been ill-founded in some ways but it was genuine at the time). The best nineteenth-century music is similarly confident and hopeful. The worst is as bad as the worst nineteenth-century fiction —escapist, irresponsibly intense, sentimental. Sentimentality is the evocation of emotion without the acceptance of responsibility, and the church style of the nineteenth century ruthlessly exposed the quality of so much popular (and successful) religion of the time.

The disagreeable consequence of this line of argument is this: that the time when the church musician began to recover his prestige and status was a time of musical degeneracy, and it was then that the church choir came into its own for the first time since the Reformation. So much music was "entertainment music" that the church musician and his choir found themselves before they realized it in religious show business. Especially that was true in the nonconformist and Reformed churches. Especially, I have to say, it was the case in the main American traditions of churchmanship.

At this point we will break off the argument. It will come to its conclusion in chapter 8. But we have made these references to past history because they show how our present-day problems had their origin, and therefore what is the right road by which to approach them now.

This book is not designed to answer all questions, but rather to indicate how to ask the right questions. But we may give one short example of how history throws light on a question which without that light we answer ineptly and imprecisely. This is the question of the non-Catholic choir. Choirs in churches of "our" kind have appeared for reasons which were neither liturgical nor theological, but rather social. So much we have seen. If we ask what is the *raison d'être* of the Reformed choir, it is wise to remember this; it is also helpful to remember that there is nothing sacrosanct about the customary functions of choirs in modern Reformed churches. Again—what they could do if they abandoned certain customs which are not of theological principle at all will be shown in chapters 6 and 8. Sometimes a choir has a very clear function—such as the massed voices that lead the singing at an evangelistic campaign. The *raison d'être* is less easy to find when a Reformed church has a choir too small to lead congregational singing, and perhaps not capable of singing anthems in a musically acceptable manner. Or if the choir can sing anthems well, what are anthems for anyway? When nonconformist choirs rose to their height of prosperity and influence in the English nineteenth century, anthems were glorified hymns—everybody joined in, and their words and music were included in the hymnals. But the place of the strictly professional anthem of the modern kind in our services need debating; it is historically dubious, and most certainly it should not be regarded as unchallengeable.

What Is Sacred Music?

On the other hand, history provides many valuable clues to the even more pressing question—what is sacred music? In our time the great theological conversations are being centered on the questions, how the holy is related to the material, how God is related to his world, how the church is related to secular society. The musical mode of the conversation is—how sacred music is related to secular music. Since it is not possible to be an effective and creative church musician without having faced that conversation and taken some part in it, even if the part one takes is no more than making up one's mind where one stands, let us see if we can summarize the help that history has so far given us.

1. In the Middle Ages there was a clearly distinguished "church style." Plainsong was "church music," rhythmic dance-like music was "secular." A broad generalization, this, but near enough for our purposes.

2. Luther, like his Protestant predecessors, made much use of secular styles in the music he encouraged; the hymn tunes were very much like the style of nonchurch music current in the later Middle Ages.

3. Calvin, through his severe discipline, developed a *new* "church style." Although Bourgeois, his musician, used

45

secular *subject matter* in his psalm tunes, the *manner* in which they were to be sung and the fact that they were so few in number and all in one style solidified a new church style which was partly a way of performing music, partly a way of composing it—a congregational and strictly unison style.

4. The English and Scottish psalm tunes reflected this "church style" and "church manner" in a simpler and more popular, but certainly not secular, form.

5. The church music of the period 1660-1740 swung right over to the secular styles of dance music and courtly music; that of the immediately succeeding period borrowed its style from eighteenth-century opera. The interest in church music of very highly qualified musicians during the period 1660-1750 helped "baptize" secular styles without any sense of incongruity.

6. The next two generations (say 1780-1850) saw a degeneration of the new secular style into a new church style through the inability of church musicians to handle the new resources as skilfully as their predecessors had handled them.

7. The rise of part singing and choral societies, together with the romantic movement in music, gave an opportunity for new secular styles to be incorporated in church music, which again, as under 6, was largely missed through the ineptitude of church musicians. The result was a church style of conspicuous sentimentality and cheapness.

8. —So what happens in the twentieth century?

Historically, we have moved from a period (the Middle Ages) in which the church style was "church" because it was being handled by the best musicians to a period in which the church style was recognizably church because it was being handled by the worst ones. At the beginning the musicians were churchmen. At the end they were increasingly not only laymen but agnostics. Earlier, the church could claim to have the most flexible, expressive, and sophisticated music there was in the West. By 1900 it was a museum of the worst music.

This is to say that, while in the earlier period church music was the best of music, in the later period church music was its best when it listened to secular music, and when the church musicians could handle secular music.

Misuse of the Secular

Now take it from another angle of view. When church music was the best music, the church had enough confidence not to feel that it needed to listen to musicians *qua* musicians. If they were churchmen they were able to read, write, and think; if they were not, they could at best be popular entertainers, folk artists. The church style of the post-Reformation era (periods 3 and 4 above) remains healthy, hard-wearing, and good because there still was not very much music about of other kinds. What there was, was music of a high quality, well tailored to its purpose of domestic singing or secular dancing. There was no large deposit of popular, cheapened music competing with church songs for the affections of ordinary people. Church music was church music partly, as we said, because of the way it was sung—congregationally and in unison and unaccompanied; polyphony, instrumental accompaniments, and solos were left to secular music. The two did not compete; they ran in parallel. It was the development of music as an independent art which raised the problems. The secular musician, after Haydn, was no longer willing to play second fiddle to the church. The secular musicians lived lives which were were diminishingly influenced by the church. Fewer really able musicians were found wholly within the church. So "secularization" becomes increasingly a matter of *misusing the secular,* and the distinction of the church style, instead of being, as it was in Palestrina's time, an excellence, became a degeneracy. Church music became bad secular music, bad simply because the musicians within the church could not handle the resources they took over. Again, this is a broad generalization, but the evidence is overwhelming.

Very well. What is the position in the present century? The position is that for some reason there has been a dramatic change in the quality and outlook of the musicians who have served the church. The old degenerate music persists at the popular level. Any hymnal editor knows how much he is bound to allow for this against his own desire to provide what he believes to be the best in music and words.

But what has happened historically, I think, is this: that (1) musicians have, through a revival of literary taste,

47

especially in Britain, been attracted by the suggestiveness of Christian *texts* even when they did not wholly or even at all subscribe to the beliefs that lay behind them, and (2) a loosening-up of the church's cultural terms of reference in Britain has undoubtedly led the first-class secular musician to believe that he will be less unwelcome as a temporary servant of the church than he formerly thought he would be. It really is significant that, whereas the great nineteenth-century continental musicians hardly ever gave of their best to the church and found little demand anyhow for many outside settings of the Mass, a composer such as Benjamin Britten is not only able to give of his best to church music but finds a demand for church music in all sorts of styles, as one can see if one lays alongside one another his *Missa Brevis,* his *Rejoice in the Lamb* and his *Hymn to St. Peter.*

Other commentators have remarked on the new attitude of composers to texts in the twentieth century. Nearly all nineteenth-century anthems were settings of verses from the psalms: relatively few were taken from elsewhere in the Bible (S. S. Wesley was one of the most literature-conscious of biblical musicians). In the days around and following 1900, the days of Parry, Stanford, and Charles Wood, there was an increasing tendency for composers to set extra-biblical sacred poetry to music. Once composers felt free to do this, it became possible for nonorthodox composers, and even non-Christian ones, to write what appears to be "sacred music." They could even approach the liturgical texts in a quite fresh and uncommitted spirit. Michael Tippett's staggering *Magnificat* (1961) is a typical example of an agnostic composer's illumination of a Christian text.

Fear of the Secular

If it is a subtle change in the church's attitude to secular culture that has produced a vast improvement in the standards of church music, both of performance and of composition, then we shall expect to find that in those parts of the church in which secular culture is least respected, improvement will have lagged and a degenerate church style in music and in the other arts will prevail. This is exactly what we do find. Without relaxing my vigilant care to avoid value judgments in this part of what I write, I can

48

quite fairly point to the familiar fact that in highly and exclusively evangelical circles in Britain taste in music is conservative. Conservative here means "addicted to nineteenth-century models," since it means retaining the cultural habits not of our remote ancestors but of a generation before our own. In varying degrees we can see how the retention of church styles which increasingly repel those who are sensitive to the developments in the arts is associated with a fundamentalist culture. And this must be why. For a fundamentalist culture tends to see the church more as a sheepfold than as a commando section in an army. The church's business, in the eyes of those who follow this way, is to gather people *in*. There are perfectly sound biblical precedents for this view, although some hold that there are other biblical precepts to be harmonized with this one before a true interpretation of the faith is achieved. But if the church is a sheepfold, surrounded by a wall, there is a tendency to think of all values appropriate to the world outside in the category of "thieves and robbers" or "wolves." The secular is normally played down, or even vilified, in these circles. Therefore the tendency will be for what is native to the church to be exalted over what is native to the world. But such is human nature, and so fallible are human memories, that the products, in doctrine and in art, of two or three generations ago will be regarded as "native to the church"—and when that happens there is clear error.

Nobody who points this out can expect to be popular, but history insists on its truth. It is the hymnals of the evangelical groups in the churches which preserve the church style of the late nineteenth century in much greater propostion than do those of the "liberal" groups. Among English hymn books, lay out on a table copies of *Songs of Praise* (1951), *The BBC Hymn Book* (1951), *Congregational Praise* (1951), *The Anglican Hymn Book* (1965), and *Hymns of Faith* (1964), and you will see a progressive hospitality to nineteenth-century tunes going hand-in-hand with a progressive emphasis on "evangelical" religion. If these were in a row reading from left to right, one could place the *Cambridge Hymn Book* (1967), edited by an agnostic, to the left of the whole row, and the *Billy Graham Song Book* (1954) to its right and the inverse ratio of evangelical religion to musical radicalism would be preserved.

More proof could be given, but here it is hardly necessary, of this correlation between theological and musical liberalism. It is what one would expect. And it is this about which the modern church musician must make up his mind. Certainly it is among the "liberal" groups in the U.S.A.—for example, the group for which *Hymnal for Colleges and Schools* was produced in 1956 at Yale—that church music is required to approximate to the standards of secular music; it is among the highly evangelical groups, such as the Southern Baptists, that the highest proportion of nineteenth-century church music, or music reviving that style, is in common use. And the point we made about "conservatism" just now is massively reinforced when we note a certain phenomenon in American hymnody, which is parallel to a similar one in Britain. The conservative groups are not necessarily those which make the greatest use of the really "old" hymnody of America: —the American folk-hymnody. It is not the original music, but the conservative music—music in the style of 1880—that most greatly appeals. It is, on the other hand, the liberal minds among conservative groups that are beginning to rediscover the ancient hymnody of the U.S.A. But if one wants to find it in the hymnals, one goes to such liberal books as the new *Methodist Hymnal,* not to the books in use among either American Baptists or Southern Baptists, to find it in any quantity.

The finishing touch may be put to this argument by answering the inevitable question—but what about the Mennonites? This is a highly conservative group among the American religions, and it makes wide use of the true hymnody of ancient American culture.

The answer to this involves an adjustment which corrects the perspective of what we have just been saying. The Mennonites are a conservative group indeed—ranging nowadays from groups which forbid travel by car to groups which forbid only the use of organs in church. They are "people of the origins" who have preserved intact an ancient culture in the midst of a society which has mostly advanced (or if you will, receded) from that cultural point generations ago. What then is the difference between the folk-hymn-singing Mennonites and the gospel-song-singing Southern Baptists? Why, as any Baptist would say at once and with firmness, the Mennonites are self-propagating and self-perpetuating whereas the Baptists are an evangelizing group. In other words, while the Mennonites systematically and innocently ignore the world outside the church wall, the Baptists are by tradition committed to making assaults on it. The Mennonites keep the wolves away from the sheep; the Baptists make war on the wolves.

The liberals, you might want to say if you are a Baptist, deceive everybody by saying "They aren't wolves; they're nice dogs."

Well, we are getting near the thin ice now, and perhaps it would be wise to equip ourselves with some slightly more sophisticated skating techniques before we venture further along this line. What it is fair to suggest at this stage is that this is the line to pursue if you want to make up your mind where you stand in the current debate about the sacred and the secular, and what it is fair to state as fact is that nobody can talk about "standards" in church music without involving himself in that debate.

II

THE CHURCH MUSICIAN AND HIS BIBLE

4

The Old Testament

The Word Within the Words

In what manner does the Bible help the church musician in his work? This is our next question, and perhaps it will be wise at our beginning to settle the terms of reference which I propose to observe in attempting to answer it.

This book may well fall into the hands of some who take, or appear to take, a different view of biblical authority from mine. My experience so far has indicated that cleavages on this point can be made to appear far deeper than they really are; and, while there are certain views of the Scriptures with which I am afraid I cannot offer any kind of compromise, I think that there will not be many who find my presuppositions here wholly untenable.

The position from which I begin is quite simply explained. I hold that any question of any importance that a man wishes to ask concerning the moral or spiritual life will be found to be answered in the Bible, but that it will not be answered necessarily by direct instruction. I cannot hold that the translation of the Scriptures published in the year 1611 is itself "the word of God," for this must mean that the Greek original of the New Testament is not the word of God, nor the Hebrew original of the Old Testament, which is manifest nonsense. Moreover, when the translation of 1611, or any other translation, can be shown to be based on a misreading of the original, I cannot hold it to be the word of God. Further again, where the original is corrupt or unintelligible simply because in its most ancient forms it cannot be read (torn or crumbled documents lie behind, for example, much of Ezekiel), we cannot be sure that even it is the word of God. Nor, even if the word of God were identified with the words of the written Scriptures, could I believe that it remained the word of God if it were manifestly misinterpreted by a commentator or a preacher. And when ancient authorities for any given text differ, and it is impossible at this stage to decide which is the "right" version, where does the word of God lie then? (This is a question which, for example, comes up conspicuously in the reading of Luke's Gospel.)

But I have to go beyond this and confess that I do not believe that the word of God, which I believe to be within the words of the Scriptures, comes to us only through the channel of *instruction*. I am sure that it is a mistake to believe that it does. This mistake has led so many innocent people to dismiss the Old Testament almost totally as being useless for the Christian life; it has led to this because they have been allowed to believe that, because men killed one another in Old Testament times in the belief that they were doing the Lord's will, we are now being instructed to kill people in the name of the Lord. I have, indeed, been impressed in my visits to the U.S.A., even more than in my travels in Britain, by the ignorance of the Old Testament which many Christians there believe to be no matter for shame.

It is necessary to abandon the notion that the Scriptures are there merely for our instruction, or, if "instruction" must be insisted on, then we must at least say that this instruction is not communicated merely by the statement of historical facts and the laying down of moral principles. It is communicated much more by *example*. The Old Testament especially is a story of God's dealings with men; to use it as though everything that men did and said was right and needed no correction by God is to miss its whole point. And yet constantly we hear people quoting as moral precepts texts from the Old Testament which are designedly human utterances, placed over against the justice and the grace of God.

The other consequence of misusing the Bible through too much reverence is the belief that if something is not mentioned in the Bible, there is no help to be gained from

53

the Bible on that subject. Some go even further and say that the subject is not worth considering. Now in the matter of church music we need to notice the damaging effects of this kind of misuse. The Bible says virtually nothing about church music. I am about to show that what it does say is of great assistance to us in determining the decisions we have to make in church music. But the Bible can do that without specifically mentioning church music. What we have suffered from for several generations now is the consequence of believing either that the Bible cannot help us, or that church music is a second-rate subject because the Bible does not mention it. All we can manage is to quote a few pleasant-sounding texts, such as "O worship the Lord in the beauty of holiness" (which does not mean what most people think it means), or "Sing ye praises with understanding" (which is a tentative reconstruction of an original that nobody has yet interpreted with any certainty). So much of our church practice in music is thoroughly untheological and unprincipled, even when we decorate it with texts such as these, that it is time we revised our notions of its connection with the ground of our faith. It is in the belief that the Bible is not to be rejected because of its elusiveness, but that it is to be wrestled with until the real meaning comes out of its pages, that I write what follows.

The Old Prophets

At an early stage sacred music in the Old Testament is associated with prophetic ecstasy. That music itself was regarded as a normal accompaniment of life from the beginning of human consciousness is attested by the ascription of its origin to Jubal in Genesis 4:21. There music is placed alongside the blacksmith's trade (vs. 22) and the customs of nomadic peoples (vs. 20) as one of the traditional and immemorial activities of mankind. But more specifically, when we get to Exodus 15 we find a new dimension in this ancient art. It is there written that, at the climax of Israel's deliverance from Egypt, the people, including Moses and (vs. 20) led by Miriam, sang a war song beginning "Sing unto the Lord, for he has triumphed gloriously." And we note that this was accompanied with "timbrels and dancing." This is the first "sacred song"—song associated with religious faith—in the Old Testament, and probably one of its very oldest documents. There is another one in Judges 5, in which the song leaders were Deborah and Barak.

Now turn to I Samuel 9 and 10. Here we are at a later stage, but still a primitive one, in Israel's history (very roughly, 1000 B.C. as against the thirteenth century B.C.). Here we read the strange story of how Israel's first king was appointed. We read in chapter 8 how the people demanded a constitutional ruler in place of the "judges," the popular heroes and demagogues, who had led them since the days of Joshua. We read how Samuel, the last of their judges, warned them that they must examine their reasons for wanting a king, and that, inasmuch as their reasons were secular and discreditable, they would regret their choice in the generations to come. The people were unmoved by this warning, and it was Samuel's duty to find the king whom they would accept. In the succeeding paragraphs of this intensely penetrating and spiritual story we find how Samuel, guided by God at every stage, found Saul—"a handsome young man" (9:2)—a man who without doubt would appeal to the people at all levels of their political consciousness. His undoubted ability and distinction of character would commend him to the more responsible, but his superficial beauty and impressiveness would blind them to the instability and weakness of his nature which later were to appear with such tragic consequences. Saul, in his beauty and his weakness, impersonated the desires, the political glory and shame, of the people he was to represent before other nations and before God.

Samuel instructed Saul, and then the people, in "the rights and duties of the kingship" (10:25), and among the things he said to Saul was that he would manifest at once certain signs of his authority and his right to govern. One of these was to be the gift of prophesy to be exact—"you will meet a band of prophets coming down from the high place with harp, tambourine, flute and lyre before them, prophesying. Then the spirit of the Lord will come mightily upon you, and you shall prophesy with them and be turned into another man" (10:5-6). And it was so (10:10), to the great surprise of everybody who stood by (vs. 11).

The point which we must notice here is the special significance of "prophecy" at this stage in Israel's development. The "prophets" were not yet the great moralists, social critics, political advisers, and preachers that they became in the days of Isaiah the First, Amos, and, later, Jeremiah. They were, says the text, primarily musicians and dancers. The ritual in which they were engaged when Saul joined them was a sort of folk ritual which, unintelligible to everybody outside it, ecstatic and esoteric in its customs, simply reminded the people of the supernatural power of their God. It hardly matters whether they themselves knew their God in anything better than a highly superstitious fashion. They were part of the religious scenery. It was surprising, it was to some hardly suitable, to find the crown prince among them.[12] But they had their uses.

They were, in fact, the artists of their time, and the notion of the prophet as folk artist develops but is never entirely extinguished. What Isaiah the First did in the delivery of his most famous message about the Lord's vineyard (Isa. 5) was to take a familiar folk song and sing it to the people—with some added verses of his own which both surprised and shocked them.[13] Isaiah the First had other parts to play in the life of Israel, but one of these was quite certainly that of the folk singer with his guitar, objectifying popular thought and then, in the true folk-song fashion, giving it a rude jerk forward toward the conclusion the singer wanted to emphasize. Folk singing and religious dance seem to have been closely associated with primitive worship in Israel—and what better confirmation of that could anybody want but the 150th psalm?

Levites

Now if one goes over the same section of Scripture again, one finds another tradition of sacred music overlaid on this ecstatic and prophetic tradition. This is the tradition of the Levites. What happens here is, as it were, the reverse of the process by which we extract our information about the prophetic tradition. In that older tradition we are seeing the end products of a primitive evolution. There were prophetic musicians, dancing dervishes of the Israelite tradition, long before there were written records; what is written about them is the description of incidents which happened to be remembered, and from those incidents we infer the existence of a tradition. But in the case of the Levites we have an enormous number of references in the early books of the Bible, and all these are from sources which were actually written quite late. They represent a reading-back into the old worship of Israel of a settled order of things which did not reach its developed form until much later than the times which are being written about.

Nonetheless for that, the Levites tell us something quite different, and complementary, about sacred music. In the book of Numbers we read the accepted account of how they came to be the hereditary organizers of Israel's worship. Apparently (Num. 16:10) the whole matter began in controversy and bitterness, but the upshot was the situation described in 18:21, "To the Levites I have given every tithe in Israel for an inheritance, in return for their service which they serve, their service in the tent of meeting." Tradition, then, had it that in the later days of the Exodus the principle was accepted that certain full-time officials should be set aside to administer worship, and that the community should support them. This is confirmed in many places—for example, Deut. 10:8, Num. 31:47.

Now whereas the Levites at the earliest stages are described as those who "had charge of the tabernacle of the Lord," or who were to "carry the ark of the covenant of the Lord" (as in the citations above), we hear in II Chronicles 5:12 of the "Levitical singers." This is at the dedication of Solomon's temple (say three hundred years after the Exodus). Moreover, we hear of certain subsections of the tribe of Levi to which the performance of music was traditionally entrusted. "David also commanded the chiefs of the Levites to appoint their brethren as the singers who should play loudly on musical instruments, on harps and lyres and cymbals, to raise sounds of joy." (I Chron. 15:16.) Among these "brethren of Levi"—members, we should say, of subbranches of the family—we especially encounter the names of Asaph, Heman, and Korah. The singers are specified as "sons of Asaph" in such places as II Chron. 35:15 and Ezra 2:41 and 3:10. Heman comes up at I Chron. 6:33 and II Chron. 29:14. Korah appears at a slightly later stage—in I Chron. 6:22 and in certain of the titles of the psalms (for which see below, p. 74).

All this is becoming somewhat an[_] We will not pursue the hundreds o[_] and their musical associations to say that it adds a touch of piquancy to the parable of the good Samaritan to reflect that it may just conceivably contain the only known reference made by our Lord to a church musician.

What matters for us is this: that in the ancient traditions concerning sacred music in Israel you have two clear lines of guidance. On the one hand, it is accepted, in the prophetic tradition of song, that sacred music is something ecstatic, inspired, topical; it is associated with dancing and with a kind of high intoxication with religion; its great symbolic figures are the flawed genius of Israel's ambition, and David, the adventurer-king of Israel's glory. Sacred music has its roots in human life with all its tragedy and all its brilliance—in Saul the beautiful and Saul the insane, in David the serene young singer who could cast out Saul's devils (but not for long; compare I Sam. 16:23 with I Sam. 18:10-11) and in David the arrogant autocrat who shamed himself with Bathsheba. (And think also of the implications of David calming Saul's frenzy with music, and of Saul later saying, "I'll stick him to the wall with my spear if he won't give over playing that guitar.") That is one tradition of sacred music.

The other is the tradition of order and liturgy, the tradition of Levi and Asaph and Heman—of men who are merely names in the biblical records. What do any of us know of Levi and Asaph, compared with what we know of Saul? Here is impersonal, legislative, liturgical music. Here is music full of religious joy and splendor, no doubt, but professional, tamed, *sacred*. Its genius is not in common life but in the holiness, the separateness, of worship.

These two remained side by side. In the psalms, as we shall see in a moment, the two natures of sacred music are fully joined and harmonized. It is error to try to see sacred music either without its Levites or without its prophets. Indeed, there is an even deeper theological principle here. For in all mortal life, where it is creative, we have to harmonize the ecstatic and the disciplined. This is something of which we have warning on the very first page of the Bible. There we learn, in that incomparable poem on the Creation, that, on the one hand, "the Spirit of God was moving over the face of the waters," and on the other, that "id, 'Let there be light'; and there was light." The juxtaposition of those two phrases in the second and third verses of Genesis 1 gives you all the poetry and passion of the universe once you take the two phrases together. On the one hand, there is God reducing chaos ("the deep") to order, bringing reason and peace out of primeval confusion —thus the poet sees it. The next moment there is God saying, "Let there be light"—bringing into being all the primal energy of the universe by a single creative word. Creation is, viewed from one point of view, an explosion of inspiration; viewed from the other, it is the reduction of anarchy and chaos to order. Any artist will tell you that both these things are true. And so will anybody who considers the necessities of Christian worship.

By noticing this magnificent counterpoint in primitive Old Testament faith, then, the musician is warned that he will never be free of the need to hold in balance the notions of order and of inspiration. The churches are still in controversy over ways of worship. Some prefer worship to be highly inspirational; some prefer it to be highly ordered. Some err in one direction, some in another. If controversy is laid aside and friendship and reciprocal courtesy are substituted, the result can be a blending, varied for different times and places and cultures, of the necessary elements of inspiration and order, and it is always necessary for any musician in any tradition to become aware of the values which his opposite number, in a tradition of the opposite kind, values. It is unwise for a Southern Baptist always to regard an Anglican Episcopal as a man of superstition because he uses a prayer book, or for the Anglican to call the Baptist as vulgarian because he does not observe Sexagesima. A living faith in any religious community depends on the creative collision of apparently opposing forces; that is always true. Never become unneighborly or bigoted. If either a preacher or a musician yields to this temptation, by his fruits he will be recognizable as a man imperfectly equipped to cope with the demands of his high calling.

The Judgment on Sacred Music

The reference we made to the parable of the good Samaritan a little while ago was by no means frivolous. There is an altogether different aspect of the Old Testament's teaching

59

about church music which must now be attended to. Its most trenchant expression is in the fifth chapter of Amos, in a passage of sacred invective, unequalled in the whole Bible, whose closing verses are these:

I hate, I despise your feasts,
    and I take no delight in your solemn assemblies.
Even though you offer me your burnt offerings and cereal offerings,
    I will not accept them,
and the peace offerings of your fatted beasts
    I will not look upon.
Take away from the noise of your songs;
    to the melody of your harps I will not listen.
But let justice roll down like waters,
    and righteousness like an ever-flowing stream (vss. 21-24).

It is one of the less delightful characteristics of the religiously zealous that they affect to hold in contempt people who take trouble over such details as church music, but I do not feel obliged to think that the prophet Amos was one of those. When he says that in certain circumstances the finest church music can be not an honor offered to God but an insult, he must be listened to patiently. For it is possible for an enthusiasm for one side of religion, such as church music, to become obsessive and to crowd out that broad and neighborly compassion that should be found in all truly religious men.

Personally, I get a great deal of pleasure out of the company of fellow church musicians. I have always enjoyed the shop-talking fellowship of organists, who resemble so much the old-fashioned railway societies of Britain (do they have those in the U.S.A.?); conversation is amiably technical, and a Saturday afternoon spent trying out some fine organ in the district is a Saturday afternoon well spent among such friends. But naturally such a fellowship can become somewhat inbred and exclusive. It is not a very good thing for a man to be interested in nothing in the world but organs (or railways).

And when you get to Amos' level, you have to admit that there are basic concerns common to all who truly profess the faith over which nothing takes priority. The organist who is obsessed with church music is not a good musician, and the musician who is obsessed with music is not a good artist, and the artist who is obsessed with art is not a good man. Somehow the Christian life demands a careful distinction between commitment and obsession. Without doubt the people against whom Amos was protesting were committed people, but they were also obsessed—obsessed with the externals of religion. They were capable of simply not noticing when their religious profession was at odds with their personal practice and their politics. Art must not be an escape from the demands of neighborly life, nor must music, nor must church music. You cannot love God, as the Epistle of John insists, if you have neglected to love your neighbor.

This is all very difficult. Suppose your neighbor is not a musician; suppose he is a philistine, a music-hater, a man who "knows what he likes"—what then? Once we have opened up that field, we are in the thick of the pastoral jungle. This is no place to begin a discussion of the artist's duty—although elsewhere I should be only too happy to argue that it differed only in inessentials from the Christian's duty—but it is surely clear that there is a side of the music minister's work which is wholly concerned with *people,* and that it is a fatal limitation to suppose that it is concerned only with ideas.

I do not here want to be agreed with too easily. I had better say at once that I do not think we have answered Amos if we say, "But we believe that church music is first and foremost an instrument of evangelism." The fallacy should be easy enough to detect. The Levites might have answered Amos by saying, "But our temple music is done to the glory of God." Amos would have replied, "That is what I complain of. You have forgotten *people.*" It is unfortunately true that one can even be a quite powerful evangelist—adept at the techniques of persuasion, free with citations from the Bible—and still forgetful of *justice* and of what Amos called *righteousness.* It will not be an adequate answer to Amos if we claim to be evangelical but have no respect for reason (of which justice is a function). It we cannot distinguish between the evangelism which merely proves that *we are right* and the evangelism which proves that *God loves the world,* we are in no condition to stand up to the thunderings of Amos. What is more, our church music will be of the kind which both displays the degeneracy of our theological thinking and encourages others to imitate that degeneracy.

The answer to Amos lies, I fancy, along only one line. If a church musician seeks to be a good musician, to train good musicians, to serve God with good music, because he believes that this is a way of loving mankind and loving God, he is clear of the indictment. If he either seeks the best music in order to show himself better than other musicians and than the unmusical, *or* seeks and performs the worst music in order to pursue and achieve the worldly success of religious show business, then he is guilty. This is not a picture; it is a diagram. It has no personal references whatever. It merely exposes the motives which in all church musicians are to some extent mixed. The message which Amos leaves with us is not that every church musician should be a political fanatic, but that he should see his work in the context of ministry to human beings and make his judgments not merely on theory but with due regard to the demands of what Christians insist on calling "love."

Nehemiah

There are points here which we shall amplify later on. But this is the stage at which we can move on to another field of thought, opened up to us by the story of Nehemiah. The question which we now want to ask is, what is the nature of the spiritual discipline of the church musician? How does he train himself not only in music but in the spiritual graces that make him a true Christian minister of music?

Here is Nehemiah's story, very briefly. Nehemiah was a Jew, living about 450 B.C. This was a time of great spiritual depression in the history of Israel. A hundred and fifty years before, the nation had suffered the worst disaster in all its history before A.D. 70—the deportation to Babylon under the legendary Nebuchadnezzar. The exact date was 586 B.C., and the story can be pieced together by reading the closing chapters of the second book of Kings and material between chapters 30 and 45 of Jeremiah. After fifty years of exile the descendants of the original deportees were allowed to return to Jerusalem; the reason for this was the sack of Babylon by Cyrus of Persia. The edict of release was a most liberal act—foreseen in the remarkable prophecies of Isaiah the Second ("Cyrus, my shepherd," Isa. 44:28). But the leaders of the returning party were people who had never seen Jerusalem. The people who had kept the old religion alive in exile found it extraordinarily difficult to arouse any enthusiasm for the restoration of Jerusalem to her former glory, even in those religious matters in which this was still possible. The plain physical operation of rebuilding the temple was delayed and pursued without zeal. This we read in the book of Haggai, and there are references to it in Zechariah 6 and 7.

Two generations later, the city wall was still in ruins, and this is where Nehemiah makes his appearance. He was, it appears (Neh. 1:1-2), a Jew with an influential government appointment in Susa, the capital of Persia (and therefore the capital of the empire of which the Jews were now a part). He asked the king whether he could be appointed to oversee the reconstruction of Jerusalem, and the request was granted.

The first task was to rebuild the city walls, and the story of this in Nehemiah 4 and 6 is one of the Old Testament's great adventure stories. The conviction in Nehemiah's mind that the rebuilding of the walls would give a much-needed boost to Jewish morale was amply confirmed by the opposition which the project encountered from their jealous neighbors in Samaria. Taunts and threats came from Samaria, designed to discourage the builders, but Nehemiah's superb administration succeeded in getting those walls built in an incredibly short time, and the Samaritans had to eat their words. (They never forgave the Jews for this, as certain passages in the Gospels remind us.)

Having completed the work on the walls, Nehemiah then proceeded to phase 2 of his reform. He called the people together and made them listen to an exhortation based on a ceremonial roll call of the names of all the families who had returned from Babylon. All this is recorded in chapter 7. But this was only a curtain-raiser. The next general gathering was called to hear Ezra the priest read "the book of the law" (8:3). There stood Ezra in a special wooden pulpit erected in the city center and read to them. He read, we must suppose, very much what we ourselves read in the first five books of the Bible: the stories of creation, of man's fall, of the patriarchs, of the exodus, and of the giving of the law.

Nehemiah knew the art of "production." He set the chief priests around Ezra at different levels, and the people stood for the reading; then, when the reading was done, special preachers were appointed to expound it (8:7-8). Finally Nehemiah himself spoke to them, and this was a truly evangelical occasion. He called for decisions; he called for action. He said, in effect, "You have heard your history; you have heard how God dealt with your fathers; above all, you have heard that your fathers were closest to God when they were in the wilderness. You shall remind yourselves now, and every year at this time, of the way in which God met your fathers in a place where they had no city, no home, no place of rest. You have your city walls; you have your national pride; you have all you need in the way of security. Now you shall all build yourselves huts or tents or booths, and leave your homes, and live for a few days in the way in which your fathers lived in the wilderness. And God will speak to you."

This was the founding of the Feast of Tabernacles, of which we hear in John's Gospel (7:2). That great festival had many overtones; it was a festival before the time of Nehemiah—the harvest festival and the covenant festival. But now also it was the festival of pilgrimage, the festival of insecurity. It taught the people, once they had achieved security, never to forget the value of insecurity. For city walls could shut out more than a human enemy; they could, through the encouragement of nationalism and narrowness and materialism, shut out God.

Here is a vital spiritual principle. It was always central to the religion of Israel in the Old Testament. There is no end to the implications of the Exodus in that religion. The Exodus itself was Israel's Easter—the most authentic sign they had in their history of God's favor and love and power. The succeeding generation of wandering left an ineffaceable mark on Israel's religious consciousness. "Strangers and pilgrims" was their key phrase. The principle is taken over unchanged into the Christian ethic; there is a certain kind of false assurance and security with which the Christian is never allowed to have anything to do. See, for example, Hebrews 11:9-10 for the most famous vindication of that, but the whole of the Sermon on the Mount is a pilgrim's ethic, and the whole controversy between our Lord and his opponents of the religious establishment was over the question of moral security. The sort of security that says that a work of mercy is evil if done on the Sabbath is the sort of security which is forbidden to Christians.

The church musician can be grateful for this teaching, even when it seems to be disconcerting. To be a Christian minister of music he must always be vigilant against the temptation to build walls that have no business being there: walls between the highbrow and the lowbrow, walls between the plain man and the intellectual, walls of contempt, walls of neglect. There is a world of difference between the obedient disciple and the doctrinaire. Many musicians vitiate their work because they are too sure what is good music and what is bad music. All this kind of false assurance does is to create divisions between people who love Tallis and people who love jazz. Again, a church musician with a good choir can become impatient of the vulgar demands of the congregation. Many very accomplished church musicians who are at their best with a twelve-part composition by Gabrieli are at their worst with a congregational hymn. Many musicians who are excellent at making a large crowd sing an evangelical chorus are helpless—even arrogantly negligent—when confronted with the demands of the intellectual or sensitive.

Moreover, there is a real danger in being blessed with too efficient a musical establishment. It is certainly not true in Britain that the churches with the best choirs are musically the most progressive or sensitive. Again and again I could recite the history of a church which forty years ago had a choir of forty voices, and now has a choir of ten, and in such churches I could show that in the days of the prosperous choir the music was complacent and conservative and geared to the preferences of people of very limited social or aesthetic sense, while in the days of adversity the music has become more congregational, more experimental, more free from obstinate traditions of style.

In Britain, indeed, we have had to learn Nehemiah's lesson the hard way, where we have learned it at all. There are places where the disappearance of a musical establishment has set music free from the dictatorship of the mediocre. I am bound to ask whether in the U.S.A., where things are still so much more prosperous and efficient, it is necessary to wait for a religious recession in order that music may be liberated? My impression is that this need not be so; it will not be so if the musicians take the lead in cultivating a religious scepticism about security. As soon as you regard security as your right, you are out of the game. Regard it as a gift, learn voluntarily to surrender it, judge music always by other standards than whether when you first hear it you like it, arouse a sense of spiritual discipline in choir and congregation, and the results, according to Gospel promises, will be unfailingly rich.

5

The Psalms in the Church Musician's Devotion

Any afternoon between 1925 and 1935, two men might have been seen walking over the downs of Sussex—bare, rolling hills, smoothly turfed, ideal for walking—enjoying animated conversation. One was a short, florid man with an ugly, good-natured face, the other a tall, lean, silent character. They were the classics master and the school doctor from a large residential school near by. The Latin master was cheerfully musical in a conservative way; the doctor played the bassoon exceedingly well in the school orchestra. You would have been surprised if you had caught a snatch of their conversation, for it would have proved to be entirely made up of quotations from the psalms. This was one of their favorite pastimes. On a slippery November afternoon it would have been like this:

L. M.: Nevertheless, my feet were almost gone; my steps had well nigh slipped. (Ps. 73:2 KJV.)

D.: (extending a strong arm) Thou hast delivered my soul from death, mine eyes from tears, and my feet from falling. (Ps. 116:8 KJV.)

Or, protesting against the school chaplain's high-church practices in chapel, including processions on saints' days:

D.: Thine adversaries roar in the midst of thy congregations, and set up their banners for tokens. (Ps. 74:4 BCP.)

L. M.: But unto the ungodly God saith, Why dost thou preach my laws, and takest my covenant in thy mouth; whereas thou hatest to be reformed, and hast cast my words behind thee? (Ps. 50:16-17 BCP.)

The legend was that they could go on like this, from one subject to another, for hours. These pious men are both dead now, and one wonders whether they have any successors. They belonged to the tradition of the Church of England and attended daily a place of worship where the psalms were sung or read "in course"—a psalm or a set of psalms, in turn, each day. Nobody could have been less monkish, or withdrawn from the world, than either of them. They were just typical of people who took pure pleasure in the psalms; for behind their witty adaptations of psalm texts to situations which would have surprised the psalmists lay a profound and detailed knowledge of the whole psalter which could have been achieved only through a profound love of it.

A hasty liberalism, in which there is little liberality, has conspired to withdraw the psalter from the worship of ordinary Christians. What the liberalism which has no sense either of poetry or of history has not wholly achieved has been completed by modernists, anti-medievalists, and, I regret to add, the misplaced pedantries of church musicians. The removal of the psalms from public worship has, I would venture to judge, been caused by

(1) the abandonment of daily liturgical services in which the psalms were read or sung with ruthless regularity,

(2) the notion that the Old Testament is not good enough for Christians to read, and can therefore be safely ignored,

(3) the real difficulty of singing the prose versions of the psalms congregationally, because of

(4) the reformed prejudice against the only really simple way of singing them congregationally—plainsong.

I shall not here discuss methods of singing; they are for others to handle in future articles. I merely state the more obvious reasons why among practicing Christians (letting alone those who have no churchmanship) hardly a hundredth part of the psalter is familiar ground.

I think that if the church musician wants to develop his appreciation of the psalms, and thereby to infect others with a love of the psalter, his best line of approach is to read them himself, to read and read until they have become part of his life. What the church will not do for him (unless he is a practicing Anglican who follows a rule of life), he can at least do for himself to the extent of reading the psalms every day, and as good a way of doing this is to read them according to the old traditional monthly lectionary. This can be found in any prayer book or Anglican psalter. I need not copy it out here, because all it entails is dividing the psalter up into sixty sections, corresponding to the thirty days of the usual month. The first is read on the first morning, the second on the first evening, and so on until the psalter is completed on the thirtieth evening. (Liturgy demands that in a thirty-one-day month the last two sections be read or sung again; you may as well spend a thirty-first day reading the great Gospel canticles—Te Deum and Benedictus in the morning, Magnificat and Nunc Dimittis in the evening.)

This course I recommend with perfect seriousness. A pocket psalter can be read in the subway; a really pleasant edition (treat yourself to one) can be read at home. Work out your divisions as you please; they may not exactly correspond to the old Anglican ones, but they will come near enough. Psalm 78 (fifteenth evening) will need an evening or a morning to itself. Psalm 119 will probably need two and a half days. It is very convenient if Psalms 120-34 can be got through in a morning and an evening. But never mind how you do it.

Which version should you use? The King James Bible or the version in the English Prayer Book (substantially Coverdale, 1538) will do admirably. These are the versions to start on. Modern ones we will deal with in a moment.

What will happen when you begin to do this? Well, if you are not careful, you will find yourself in deep water at an early stage, and you will want to swim for the shore. A great deal of what is written in the old versions of the psalms is difficult to understand. What are you to do about this?

I offer the shocking advice—at the early stages, don't worry. Read through the difficult passages; don't slam the book shut in despair; leave them in suspension until you have got to the end. Leave them in suspension until you have gone through the psalter many times, and have really got to know well at least a part of it. It's one thing to read only Psalms 23 and 46 and 84 and 103 because they are beautiful. It is quite another thing to come upon their beauties in sharp juxtaposition to the terrors of Psalm 22, the rich oriental lushness of Psalm 45, the monstrous hatreds of Psalm 83, the tribal barbarities and splendors of Psalm 102. Reading the psalter and really encountering its light and shade, its ups and downs, its valleys and mountains, is something much more like the pilgrimage of life than just taking the parts of it that most evidently appeal to what we are pleased to call our religious minds.

Be in no hurry to unravel the mysteries, to get to the bottom of the problems. The point here is that if you simply leave out Psalm 49 because it's not one of the famous ones, or because some of it is obscure, this is what you will miss:

Be not thou afraid, though one be made rich, or if the glory of his house be increased;
For he shall carry nothing away with him when he dieth, neither shall his pomp follow him.

If you avoid Psalm 78 because it looks long (it is a good deal shorter than most short stories), you will miss this:

They spake against God also, saying, Shall God prepare a table in the wilderness?
He smote the stony rock indeed, that the water gushed out, and the streams flowed withal; but can he give bread also, or provide flesh for his people? . . .
Man did eat angels' food; for he sent them meat enough.

After much exploration of modern translations, I believe that the best advice is to read the Psalms in one of the old versions first; there is nothing like them for catching one's attention with haunting phrases and memorable rhythms. Read and read and read; read slowly, hearing the words, not in the modern fashion, whole paragraphs at a time. This is the beginning of the road. Then three new fields wait to be explored.

The first is to unravel the difficult phrases, and to get below the shimmering surface of the words toward their real meaning. Both this and the second process are designed to that end, but the first is to read a modern translation. The translations I venture to recommend are either that of Ronald Knox, which is published separately in a handily small book, or the Grail translation published by Fontana Books in a paperback called *The Psalms: A New Translation*. The second of these preserves the Hebrew rhythms with great faithfulness and translates the Hebrew into very simple English. Both these translations are of Roman Catholic provenance, and the reader has to remember that in the Roman Catholic church a different numbering of the psalms is followed from that to which Protestants are accustomed: from Psalm 9 through Psalm 145 each psalm bears a number one lower than in the Protestant Bibles ("our" Psalm 23 is Psalm 22 for Roman Catholics), except in the area Psalms 114-17, where the numbering compares as follows:

Protestant	Roman
113	112
114 ⎱	113
115 ⎰	
116	⎰ 114
	⎱ 115
117	116

The revised psalter published in 1966 in England gives a very good conservative revision for those who want an alternative.

This will clear up obscurities in the actual language of the old versions. You will learn that "seek after leasing" in Psalm 4:2 means "seek after falsehood." You will learn that "Thou shalt convert my soul" in Psalm 23 means "Thou shalt refresh my soul." This will get you one stage deeper into the meaning of the psalter.

But there will still be major questions left unanswered, for you may well be still wondering what sort of use it is to read, in a supposedly sacred source, exhortations to take Babylonian children and dash their heads against stones (Ps. 137), or the strange oath uttered by some angry Hebrew against an offending neighbor, "his bishopric let another take." You may have learned that "grin like a dog and run about the city" in Psalm 59 means, "run, hungry as dogs, about a city of famine," but you may still want to know who is supposed to be interested in that thought.

There is only one answer to this: that is, to become acquainted with enough background history to be able to catch the major references in the psalms. This is not to invite every church musician to become an Old Testament scholar or to learn Hebrew; it is no more than to invite him to ask the questions which anybody reading any book intelligently is liable to ask, and then to put him in the way of finding the answers. After all, you can to some extent enjoy Perry Mason without showing any interest in the jurisdictional procedures of American law courts or the geography of Los Angeles, but you can enjoy him more if you do not insist on being uninterested in the background. The same goes for Shakespeare. Perhaps it is inevitable that we remark here that the greatest obstacle to modern man's reading the Bible profitably is his diminishing capacity for reading anything profitably, but we won't go further into that.

Basically, here are the background notions and historic facts which help you understand the psalms. Any good modern commentary will amplify them, and here we can do no more than sketch them with the greatest economy.

1. Three historical events are landmarks in the faith, as well as the history, of Israel. They are more integral to Israel's faith than the date 1776 is to American faith, because faith and politics are in the mind of Israel far less clearly separated. If you are a people with a perfectly clear understanding of a divine vocation, the things God does in history will dovetail into the things you believe about God much more than if you are a secular society, as we now are, or even than if you are a very religious society, as New England used to be. These three events are

- (a) The Exodus, Israel's "Easter," the event which gave them their national faith; about the thirteenth century B.C.
- (b) The conquest of the northern half of the kingdom by Assyria—701 B.C.
- (c) The conquest of the remainder by Babylon— 586 B.C.

Event (a) appears constantly as a pivital point in the psalms. It is the full subject matter of Psalms 78, 105, 106, and 114. It is a pivotal doctrinal point in Psalm 77—a particularly fine example of the integration of historic event with personal faith. Event (b) does not, probably, have a very important part to play in the psalms; how conspicuous it is depends on how one dates certain psalms, and in most cases dating is still quite impossible. But quite possibly Psalms 124 and 129 refer to it. However—if there is a reference to the plight of a conquered people and that reference is not to event (b), then it is certainly to event (c). Psalm 137 is the clearest reference to it, of course: and in order to get inside Psalm 137 one wants to read the closing chapters of II Kings and Jeremiah 37-45. Psalm 74 may well be another which refers to that event. If we include in event (c) the return from the Babylonian Exile, the supreme event of deliverance prophesied in Isaiah 40-55, then Psalm 80 and Psalm 126 are clearly references to it.

2. Since politics and faith were inextricably associated in Israel's thought, the king was also the priest. Many psalms refer to the enthronement of the king, and this enthronement was not merely what happened when a new king succeeded one who had died but was an annual commemoration and celebration. The notions of the king's sovereignty and service were associated with those of God's rule and redemption. That is the point of, e.g., Psalm 72, and the notion of the king as conqueror was associated with that of God as the supreme Being who was "judge among all gods"—Psalms 82, 95, 96, 97, 98, 99, 100. The fact that kings are not often to be found in modern highly developed states need not place the "enthronement" psalms far beyond our comprehension; a good deal is gained by a reintegration of political righteousness with religious faith, whatever the political pattern adopted in modern countries.

3. Israel's way of worship in the time when the psalms were written was centered on the temple; local worship was done away with in the time of Josiah (late seventh century) and only revived, in the shape of the synagogue (to which Jesus went habitually in his day: Luke 4) at a later stage. And the temple worship centered on (a) certain annual festivals which all the faithful attended, wherever they lived, and (b) sacrifice. The great holiday periods of the festivals are especially commemorated in the "psalms of ascent" or "of pilgrimage" (120-34; see especially 122), and the central sacrifices, repellent though they naturally are to modern men, represented the only way known to Israel of giving something valuable to God. To get the strength of this, one has to see that the abundant and resplendent opulence of the temple represented the dedication of monetary wealth, and the offering of a beast of sacrifice represented the dedication of the one thing more important than substantial wealth—life. Once that has been got straight, the tremendous force of Psalm 50, in which

73

materialistic views of sacrifice are ruthlessly exposed and condemned, has a chance to show itself.[14]

It is, we have said, impossible to assign dates to any but a very few of the psalms, and those only in a very generalized way. It may be taken as settled that they were not all written by David. (Would David have wept by the waters of Babylon—Psalm 137? A few may have been—people like to believe that Psalm 23 was, and nothing prevents our believing that, though nothing compels it; Psalm 18 is a direct transcription of II Samuel 22 (or the other way round); certain other psalms have traditional headings that assign them to David (e.g., Psalm 51, associated with David's repentance after the rape of Bathsheba)—but even if a few were written by him, and we cannot even assign to the traditional headings any but the flimsiest authority, certainly the authorship of the psalms as we have them is as varied and as much subject to editorial alterations as is that of the contents of any modern hymnal. There are songs elsewhere in the Bible that could have been psalms (such as Isaiah 12, and much of the poetry in Isaiah 40-55, and Habakkuk 3), and certainly many of the psalms as we have them have been reconstructed by editors who wanted to make poetry written for private purposes suitable for public worship (the last two verses of Psalm 51 are an obvious example). The psalter that we have is arranged in five sections, each of which finishes with a doxology (the sections end at Psalms 41, 72, 89, 105, and 149; Psalm 150 is a doxology to conclude the whole collection). Evidences of older sources from which they may have been taken is possibly provided in notes in the Bible headings such as "for the sons of Korah," or "of Asaph," or even "of David"—meaning, perhaps, "from Korah's book, David's book, Asaph's book." Expressions such as "upon neginoth" in the headings may refer either to means of performance or to tunes that were well known and thought suitable as companions to the psalms they are associated with.

Information of this kind can, perhaps, help a musician see the psalter not as a dim and archaic collection of tribal lays, but as a manual of faith. The essential thing to remember is that the psalms contain a distillation of that faith into which Jesus of Nazareth was born. A little wandering about in these hinterland areas will bring them to life for the reader; when this has happened, he will experience a sense of profound revelation when he associates Psalm 122:6 with Luke 19:42,[15] or Psalm 43:3 with John 8:12-36.

O pray for the peace of Jerusalem! . . .
Would that even today you knew the things that make for peace!
    . . .
Send out thy light and thy truth;
    let them lead me. . . .
I am the light of the world. . . . You will know the truth.

Remembering that the lament of Jesus would have been spoken on the first sight of Jerusalem after the long "ascent" of the hills which at holiday seasons would have been accompanied by singing the "songs of ascent" of which Psalm 122 is one, and that the great speech of Jesus was spoken at the Feast of Tabernacles, at which Psalm 43 may well have been one of many liturgical psalms (others were Psalms 81 and 118), one begins to see how far the life and public speech of our Lord may have been influenced by that part of the Bible which his hearers certainly knew better than any other except the book of Exodus. It is striking indeed to note how often our Lord makes use of the psalms, compared with the relatively little use that he makes of the redemption passages in Isaiah.

Finally, let it be remembered that, although many of the psalms in our Lord's time were used in worship, very few —only those with refrains perhaps, such as 24, 46, 99, 136—were at all commonly used *congregationally*. And this raises the point at which the church musician, having now as we hope soaked himself in the psalms for the regeneration of his own faith, turns back to their practical use in church worship of our own day.

At this point I merely wish to make certain suggestions. It is for others to go into details.

It is, of course, always right to use the psalms for the devotion of a community, as the monastic services of the Anglican and medieval Catholic churches used them. I have referred to this already. What a man can do for himself —reading the psalms right through regularly and repeatedly —a group of friends can do. The services that provide for such readings and singings are in their origin services for a group of friends—monastic services, not services of public worship.

It is equally clear that for indiscriminate public use not all the psalms are, or ever were thought by anybody to be, suitable. I have encouraged the church musician to do some close work on them; any Christian ought to do that, but where a service is "public" you can hardly expect that everybody present will have done this. Innocent or ignorant people think that singing psalms is like singing hymns—that singing aspirations or statements with which the singer wholly identifies himself. He cannot do this with many of the psalms. Therefore only a selection of the psalms—the kind of selection that many Protestant hymnals provide—is suitable for public use.

These ought to become well known, and music should be provided that makes them easy to sing. The easiest music for immediate use among Protestants is either Gélineau's psalmody, which is new, and needs to be learned (but which is very rewarding when it is learned), or metrical psalmody. I should not dream of recommending the hideous verbal carpentry of the Scottish metrical psalter to anybody who was not a thoroughly traditional Scotsman, but many good hymn-writers have versified the psalms and in doing so have distilled their central messages of adoration and praise. Hymnals usually provide good examples of these—by Isaac Watts, Henry Lyte, James Montgomery, and certain more modern writers. Among the best of these are—

O God, our help in ages past (Ps. 90—Watts)
God is our refuge and our strength (Ps. 46—Watts)
O God, thou art my God alone (Ps. 63—Montgomery)
God is my strong salvation (Ps. 27—Montgomery)
Through all the changing scenes of life (Ps. 34—Tate)
Praise, my soul (Ps. 103—Lyte)
Praise the Lord, his glories show (Ps. 150—Lyte)

There are other hymns which in a traditionally biblical way "apply" the shape of the psalmists' thought to Christian teaching—

Jesus shall reign (Ps. 72—Watts)
Hail to the Lord's Anointed (Ps. 72—Montgomery)
Out of the depths I cry to thee (Ps. 130—Luther)

And, of course, there is the traditional and magnificent Old 100th.

But again—although many psalms are hardly suitable for public praise, there is no reason why they should not be sung as solos, or choir pieces, as a kind of Bible-reading. They are matchless in their evocation of human experience and human longing. Even in their moral imperfection they can comfort us by sharing our imperfection and pointing toward God. It is here that a choir, singing an Anglican chant with that delicate precision, the lack of which makes Anglican chants so disagreeable, can really interpret scripture to a congregation, or when a soloist, singing either a bare plainsong tune or something such as Gélineau's setting of "By the Waters of Babylon," can add to the drama which the reading of the Old Testament should always inject into worship. If anyone wants to explore new dramatic forms of worship, it is in the psalms that he may well make his beginning.

This, then, is the pattern: first, get in amongst the psalms; then, find out everything that will help you see them "in the round," giving full value to every kind of human and religious experience that they handle. Then there will be no restraining the enthusiasm with which you will want to bring the psalms back into Christian worship.

6

The Psalms in the Church's Worship

If the minister of music has been aroused by reading and making friends with the psalms to use them in the church's worship, what should he do? There is no problem here if he is of the Catholic or Anglican tradition, but there are very real problems if he is of the Reformed tradition, because the Reformed use of the psalms has always been so different in its purpose and its manner from the others.

A musician will approach the question by considering first the five ways of performing the psalms which are at present available and seeing what questions arise after thinking about each one. The five methods of performance are:

1. singing to Anglican chants;
2. singing to plainsong;
3. singing to Gélineau's psalmody, or something like it;
4. singing in metrical versions;
5. reading, normally responsively.

The three purposes the psalms serve in worship are these:

a. as Bible readings;
b. as hymns;
c. as liturgical epigrams.

This we will now amplify.

The Five Methods and Their Characteristics

1. The *Anglican chant* is an elastic musical form, permitting a good deal of musical sophistication, that accommodates the combination of varying reciting length and cadence which the traditional translations of the Hebrew present as psalm poetry. A very broad spectrum of musical values can be

expressed in the Anglican chant form, and in the three
hundred years or so of its currency most of the possibilities
have been explored. It may be of ultimate musical simplicity,
such as this by Pelham Humfrey, who died in 1674:

It may be a quite sturdy congregational tune, such as
this, written only a little later:

It may be a condensation of Victorian melodrama, such
as this:

It may be a gritty twentieth-century comment such as this,
by Sydney Watson (b. 1903):

There must be thousands of Anglican chants, single and
double, available in print, and many more in manuscript.

This capacity for a great deal of musical expression within a small compass makes the Anglican chant a very good vehicle for conveying (of course, in terms of the musical age it comes from) the subtle colors of a psalm. In a long psalm a change of chant can reflect a change of mood.

But the amount of music one can get into an Anglican chant usually leads to the chant's presenting itself to the ear as a composition with an internal rhythm of its own. Since virtually all such chants come from the musical era when the bar line was an accepted convention and regular dance rhythm governed composition, it follows that the ear simply cannot help hearing most chants as rhythmical compositions in minims and semibreves. This contradicts the stress rhythm of the traditional English versions of the psalms, and in order to minimize the conflict between the musical nature of the chant and the free rhythms of the words the discipline of "speech rhythm" has been evolved by choirmasters. This is a discipline so strict and delicate as to be impossible for a generalized congregation to achieve; it involves an elasticity of rhythm not only in the allocation of syllables within the recitation but also in the moving part of the melody corresponding to the speech length of the syllables sung. A good choir singing from the *Oxford Psalter* will produce something like the following effect from Wesley's beautiful chant in G:

O how a - mia-ble are thy dwell-ings: thou Lord of hosts.

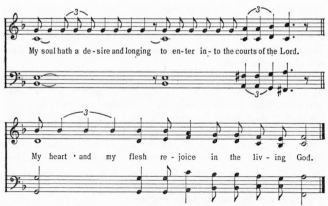

My soul hath a de-sire and longing to en-ter in-to the courts of the Lord.

My heart ˙ and my flesh re-joice in the liv-ing God.

But this is strictly chamber music; it requires great skill and constant practice, and moreover it requires a suspension of the ordinary singer's assumptions about the kind of music that the chant is using. Therefore the Anglican chant is truest to its nature when it is sung by a choir and listened to by the congregation. If there is congregational participation, a certain degree of rhythmical thump is unavoidable. These questions then arise:

a. How serious is the damage to public taste done by the congregational "thump"?

b. Is the idea that the psalms be "read to music" by a good choir and listened to by the congregation any more incongruous than the idea that any other part of the Scriptures should be read and listened to?

2. *Plainsong* is the chant form from which the Anglican chant developed. The Anglican chant was plainsong adapted to the new conventions of rhythmical and harmonized singing. Plainsong is independent of harmony and of dance rhythm and therefore has perfect qualifications for rendering elastic verbal rhythms. This elasticity is its great asset.

But plainsong is so very naïve musically (at least in the form in which we encounter it in Gregorian psalm tunes) that it has a certain undesirable effect on the worshiper unless pains are taken to counteract this. Compared with most contemporary church music (or music of any sort), plainsong suggests an almost ascetic renunciation of the pleasures of music. I say it *suggests* this; musicians, of course, delight in disciplines; people who are sated with more sophisticated music take refreshments in the severe discipline through which plainsong can make its very eloquent effects. This is all very well for musicians; the man in the pew does not always see it so.

Moreover, plainsong needs to be sung antiphonally—from side to side of an equally divided congregation, or by choir and congregation alternately, or by cantor and congregation. Plainsong thus sung becomes a very good vehicle for the massed, yet disciplined, reading of psalms to music; it is better thought of as reading-plus than as music-minus. And, when it is accompanied, the freedom of improvisation within the strict rules of modal music can be a fascinating study for the organist. The questions plainsong raises are:

a. Can you bear antiphonal singing?

b. How much music do you think the psalms need? Do you feel they can be well rendered by music so naïve as plainsong?

Possibly it is sentimental to add that plainsong almost certainly has a direct genealogical connection with the synagogue music that our Lord knew. This could, I suppose, be a possible selling point for anybody who wanted to introduce it to a congregation prejudiced against plainsong's medieval associations, but it is not an argument that should be pressed. Our Lord did not ride a bicycle or drink tea.

3. *Gélineau* is a kind of modern psalmody adapted to a new rhythmical translation of the Hebrew that preserves exactly the original meters. At present Gélineau means the work of one composer, but it could easily develop into a style, or even into a school. Unlike plainsong or the Anglican chant, it stems from a thoroughly professional root—Josef Gélineau is a first-class musician, whatever his technical status. Developments on it may turn out to be corruptions. In its present pure state its music is a cunning combination of melodic simplicity and harmonic suggestiveness. It has been published in an edition of such typographical *savoir faire* as to make it easy to teach and to pick up. It is capable of massed treatment, or of chamber music or solo treatment. Its strength lies in its unquestionable musical integrity and in the felicity of the translation (in French or English) which it uses. But it does not use the familiar versions, and some people hardly think they have sung the

psalms unless they have sung them in the Prayer Book or King James versions. Moreover, Gélineau shares one problem with plainsong: it has to be sung antiphonally. Thirdly, Gélineau makes use of the antiphons to the psalms—choruses, as it were, pointing the meaning of the psalm, variable choruses pointing different but always appropriate meanings. This (which can but does not absolutely need to apply to plainsong performance) introduces another custom which ordinary Reformed congregations are not used to, except in the very different context of the gospel song.

4. If the doctrine prevailing in any church group is that, where the congregation sings at all, it must sing all the time, the answer can only be in the *metrical psalm*. Metrical psalms, seen at their purest in Scotland nowadays, are no more than rearrangements of the biblical words in patterns that accommodate metrical tunes, almost always in the same pattern. Geneva had 110 patterns for the 150 psalms; Scotland has one for the whole psalter, with occasional alternative versions in other meters of which the Old 100th and the Old 124th are the best known. Here you have a form which is entirely easy to sing, and those who enjoy its benefits feel no sense of loss when they are required to render

> The Lord shall preserve thy going out and thy coming in
> from this time forth, for evermore

as

> Henceforth thy going out and in
> God keep for ever will.

All psalm tunes (or a sufficient number for any congregation of simple taste) are easy and well known. There is no problem of singing or, nowadays, of learning. In Scotland you can thoroughly enjoy metrical psalms if you feel that metrical psalms are a great deal better than no psalms.

But since metrical psalms go to psalm tunes, which are hymn tunes, the singing of more than six verses become exhausting, and the custom, therefore, is to sing only short portions of psalms or very short complete psalms. This, together with a certain amount of mild resistance to the grosser infelicities of the Scottish version, has produced the widespread abuse by which Scots customarily sing only a dozen psalms, which add up to little more than sixty verses of the whole psalter. The questions arising from metrical psalms therefore are:

a. Is *beauty* (such as the Prayer Book or King James versions have and the metrical psalter has not) an important factor in determining which way one will sing psalms?

b. Do you want to use psalms as hymns or as Bible readings? For metrical psalmody is indistinguishable from hymnody.

5. There remains the public *reading* of the psalms, such as is regularly done in Anglican churches where congregational singing is for one reason or another impossible and is also provided for in some American hymnals (such as the Presbyterian and Methodist hymnals). This, in order really to make its effect, has to be a kind of unrehearsed choral speech and is best performed antiphonally. In order to reflect the poetic structure of the psalms the change of voice must come at the half-verse, and this has the added advantage that a half-verse is normally brief enough to make for disciplined reading, such as dissipates itself in the course of even so short an utterance as a whole psalm verse. Where people are used to talking in church, as they are in a country parish church in England where responses and even canticles may be chorally read, psalm-reading can be a means of grace; where the custom is not followed in other parts of the service, reading becomes a rather melancholy substitute for singing. The one question that psalm-reading raises is—

Are you prepared to take choral speech seriously?

The Purposes of Psalm-Singing in Worship

Now we come to what the psalms are supposed to do in worship.

a. In the first place, psalms can be thought of as Bible-readings, appropriately read to music because they, or most of them, were designed for singing. If nearly all the psalms are used in worship, then it is essential that their performance be seen as Bible-reading, not as hymn-singing. There is a convention, quite a proper one, that in singing hymns we sing our belief. There is no such convention about reading the Old Testament. In reading it we enter into the experience of those to whom, in their imperfection, the revelation of

God came in the Old Covenant. It is essential that this be not omitted from our worship; we have already implied some of the reasons, and in our last chapter we have something to say about the way in which worship really can accommodate this experience. In the highly selective use of psalms, prose or metrical, in non-Anglican traditions and in extra-liturgical services, the psalms are used as hymns, and we sing only those which contain sentiments with which we can associate ourselves.

But as we have said, if psalms are Bible-readings, then the reading can be done as well by trained singers for the congregation to listen to as by the whole congregation —probably better. Good Anglican chants well sung, as anybody who has attended a cathedral evensong knows, are an excellent means for this kind of public reading.

b. If psalms are used as hymns, then they probably will be sung by everybody. For all sorts of reasons the antiphonal system is best, if the congregation will submit to what may be unfamiliar to their way of worship. Plainsong sensitively rendered is first-rate and simple; Gélineau is exceedingly dramatic. But in honesty perhaps one must add this: that the sturdier kind of Anglican chant is perfectly possible for congregational use to a simple psalm if you don't mind the "thump," the distortions of speech rhythm which congregational singing cannot avoid. People often object to Anglican chants because their rendering by congregations makes a disagreeable sound, but unless you are broadcasting to distant listeners, when you must be very careful not to make disagreeable congregational noises, nobody is actually listening to congregational performances at all. It is possible to be too pedantic and perfectionist when pure congregational singing is being considered, but once you are considering a listener, whether it is a congregation listening to a choir or somebody listening to a radio or television broadcast, then pedantry and perfectionism become a matter of the highest importance. It is just as well, however, to be able to distinguish the two kinds of situation.

c. What Reformed churchmen do not know enough about is the Catholic use of psalms as liturgical epigrams: that is, the use of a verse or two with an antiphon at the Eucharist or the Mass. Without going here into the details of this, we can point to the possibilities of using very short extracts from the psalms to highlight special movements of worship. The only one that is at all familiar to Protestants is the use in Scotland (in the metrical version) when the communion elements are brought into the sanctuary of Psalm 24:7-10. This is a matter which the musician, when he has considered what our last chapter has to say, may well wish to explore for himself. In the nature of things, any form of psalm-singing is as appropriate to this as any other, choral or congregational.

The Psalms as an Illumination of Worship

But what really matters here is to put the point that the psalms offer endless opportunities for the musician to share with the church the experience which, if he followed the advice of chapter 5, he has gained. Where the traditional anthem has become somewhat jaded and perfunctory, the singing of psalms could provide a freshening discipline for the choir and a quite new means of illumination for the congregation. Moreover, the custom of antiphonal singing shows the choir's part in worship in a new light. Where questions begin to be asked about the usefulness of a small choir for leading singing or the doubtful degree of edification provided by a choir constantly singing indifferent or irrelevant anthems, something quite new happens to a congregation when it has become accustomed to singing in partnership with the choir, which is what antiphony is. It is not a question of silencing the congregation so that the choir may sing; it is a matter of equal partnership. The unfolding drama of a long psalm loses all its formidable and exhausting aspects if the singing is done in partnership in this way. This is to revive a most ancient custom, but it can be revived easily and put into modern dress, as it were, if a congregation will submit to a little "production" on the part of minister and choirmaster.

But whatever the means, oh that the psalter, with its richness, its awe, its innocence, its barbarity, its humbling reminders that we are as other men are, its unexampled sense of God's majesty and beauty and compassion, were by any means brought back to the affections of all those Christian gatherings from which a too-anxious preoccupation either with aesthetic taste or with the needs of slothful congregations has so nearly extruded it in our time!

7
The New Testament

The New Testament is much more specific than the Old Testament; it is designed to show the content of our redemption in the coming of Jesus Christ, and the manner in which the work of the Holy Spirit in the church began. It is not, like the Old Testament, a picture of human life. It is a collection of documents gathered round a single event—the Incarnation of God in Christ.

For this reason it is always a mistake to use the New Testament as though it were a complete moral guidebook. It is not even a complete picture of the field in which morals operate. The Old Testament is at least that, but the New Testament was never designed to be that. There are a thousand and one subjects upon which the New Testament gives no specific guidance. The Christian's business is to infer from the New Testament statement of events a moral system consonant with obedience to the will of God there revealed.

At certain points the narrative parts of the New Testament happen to show us what was the thinking of the primitive Christians, in the light of the Resurrection, about certain specific matters. Even when it does that, the New Testament does not claim to say the last word. It is the Holy Spirit who takes of the things of Christ and shows them to us, and the New Testament is a record only of the beginning of the Holy Spirit's work in history. In other words, it is for Christians to make judgments in the light of their faith; they must not expect the judgments to be made for them in the Bible. The pattern is there in the Bible; the actual judgments must be made by men of faith as the occasion for each judgment presents itself.

There is one principle, however, which the Epistles seem to establish concerning worship, and that is that worship in the Christian community is intimately bound up with friendship. It is worth our while to examine this; it offers a certain important criticism of some of our contemporary habits.

There is a famous text which appears at Ephesians 5:19 and also at Colossians 3:16 in which Christians are exhorted to "address one another in psalms and hymns and spiritual songs" (Colossians says "admonish one another"). The context of this in both sources is an exposition of the Christian life; the author[16] of these letters is showing Christians what it is that makes the Christian life different from the life of the unbeliever. In Ephesians the whole section began at the beginning of chapter 4, with a call to manifest "lowliness and meekness, with patience, forbearing one another" (vs. 2); the unity of the church, dependent on its ascended Lord, was insisted on, and a long section following contrasts the Christian life with the the life that is given to "falsehood" (vs. 25), laziness (vs. 27), "bitterness" (vs. 31), "immorality" (5:3), and all the values of "darkness" (5:8) which "the Gentiles" follow (4:17). Just after our text there is a fine passage on the sanctity of marriage.

In the middle of all this we have this exhortation to "address one another" in music, and the immediate context in Ephesians is a warning against drunkenness. (In Colossians, it is a plea for the peace of Christ.) Without resting on a single text more weight than it was designed to bear, we may conclude that the author of these messages saw the song of the gathered company of Christians as a symbol of the unity in brotherly love and in resistance to the debased standards of the world for which they should look and which was promised to them in the ascension of Christ (Eph. 4:9). Indeed, the specific wording of the Ephesians passage brings out a point of considerable importance, for they are enjoined to speak to one another in *psalms*— which are exactly what they appear to be, the psalms of the Old Testament, in *hymns*—which we may suppose to be new compositions celebrating the resurrection of Christ (as the one from which Eph. 5:12 presumably quotes), and in *spiritual songs*. Now the spiritual songs may well be the musical equivalent of "speaking with tongues" (of which more in a moment)—the kind of improvised folk song that naturally grows out of a group which is sharply separated from the rest of society and which has a strong sense of inner unity. And the spiritual songs are contrasted with the bogus ecstasies of drunkenness. Verse 18 says, "do not get drunk with wine . . . but be filled with the Spirit." The "spirit" is, among other things, the author of that gift of supernatural expression which we must suppose to have been a special mark of the early Christian communities, and which indeed some, taking too narrow a view of this matter, and ignoring the warning we are about to quote from Paul himself, think to be an indispensable mark of Christian authenticity.

It is not the "spiritual song," in the sense of ecstatic musical utterance, that we need to emphasize here so much as the idea of music as a function of fellowship. It clearly occurred to the writer of Ephesians as perfectly natural to mention singing as the most conspicuous symbol of that fellowship which Christians were obliged to cultivate if, in those days of persecution, they were to survive. This, as we shall see, translates quite easily into our modern situation if we are not too urgent in our desire to preserve the literal sense of "speaking with tongues."

If we turn to I Corinthians 14, we do indeed learn the truth about "speaking with tongues." For there the Apostle, in a chapter which is much less often read than those on either side of it, is supporting and illustrating his argument about Christian love being the fabric of the church by specific reference to this curious manifestation. We have had reason recently to be reminded, in the new Pentecostal movement, of the nature of "tongues"; from time to time Christian gatherings have generated a habit of ecstatic and unintelligible speech, and it has been claimed by some that without this there can be no real Christian gathering. On this point the Apostle is somewhat astringent. He reminds his readers that though "speaking in tongues" may impress an unbeliever (vs. 22), it is useless if the speaker really wants to communicate anything to his neighbor. Without interpretation, speaking with tongues is useless; not only the spirit, but also the mind, must be brought into the service of Christian fellowship and communication (vss. 13-15).

And it is at this point that he catches the attention of the church musician by saying (vs. 26): "When you come together, each one has a hymn, a lesson, a revelation, a tongue, or an interpretation." In other words, the typical meeting of Christians is an occasion when each member brings something to it, to share with the rest. It is fellowship that matters, first, last, and all the time.

What the church musician can learn from this is something very simple, but in our own time easily overlooked. We are apt to forget that music in church is not necessarily a unifying influence, a function of friendship, but a divisive influence, a generator of resentment. Experience confirms it. Whenever music in a Christian community goes beyond a certain quite elementary degree of sophistication, a division appears between the "highbrows" and the "lowbrows," between the professional and the amateur, between the organ console and the pew—the pulpit becoming an uneasy and often unsuccessful mediator. There can be something of the wrong kind of speaking with tongues about church music; it can be chosen and performed without sufficient regard to the need for communication to people who have come to church for reasons that are certainly not primarily musical.

The best way to put this positively is to suggest with some firmness that it is part of the equipment of the church musician to know what it feels like to be unmusical but compelled to hear music. There is a case for saying that people who come to church bringing no musical gift but the rudimentary ability to join in well-known hymns are being shortchanged if they are faced with hymns none of which they know; or if people who have come to church expecting to hear the gospel preached are faced, without due notice, with a cantata instead of a sermon. A congregation is not a concert audience. If you don't like music, you need not go to the Metropolitan Opera. But is a defect in musical appreciation a reason for staying away from church or being made to feel inferior and underprivileged if one goes to church?

We are, of course, in danger of appearing to support the argument that all music in church should speak to the lowest level of musical intelligence. That we do not mean and must never be taken to mean. But it should be one of the marks of the church's special genius that its music can be satisfying both to the musician of fastidious standards and to the nonmusical worshiper. The spirit of I Corinthians 14:26 is best caught if the music minister in any church is sensitive to the impression that his music makes on the nonmusical and trains himself to interpret the half-articulated comments of the nonmusical so that they become creative. The spirit is lost altogether if the musician feels that if a man is not musical he brings nothing with him to worship. There is a great deal of music of the highest integrity that is part of the church's folk music; the hymnals contain much of it —even the most corrupt hymnals contain some. Begin from the common ground, and recognize what music outside that ground will win the worshiper and what will cause him difficulty. Then decide how much difficulty he can reasonably, as a Christian, be asked to encounter, and don't go beyond that limit unless there is some compelling pastoral reason for doing so. By such means, church music finds its own speed of improvement and its own means of preserving its vitality.

This could be put in another way. It is not simply the church musician's business to be improving people musically. That is best regarded as a by-product of his activity. His business is to contribute to the drama and the wholeness of that particular act of worship. Of hundreds of fine organ pieces, scores of great hymns, dozens of good anthems, he will want to choose that which is appropriate for *this* occasion, having regard to everything that makes it an occasion, including the worshipers themselves.

One of the things that can make church music divisive is the tendency of church musicians to strike attitudes. Any sensitive musician who is capable of self-criticism will know how, in his progress through the years, he has come to see how much of his criticism of music has been insincere. The progress to maturity is marked very clearly by an increasing objectivity in criticism. For example: in Britain the typical "pilgrim's progress" in music criticism has begun with a violent condemnation of everything Victorian, inspired by the very necessary warnings uttered by Vaughan Williams, Martin Shaw, Percy Dearmer, and Robert Bridges around 1900-1920. A young musician of, say, 1935-45, would regard it as immature to approve anything written in the English nineteenth century. This blanket generalization implied that nobody in the nineteenth century knew how to write music. This is manifestly nonsense; it is a sign of growth, perhaps, but not of maturity, to make such judgments. The mature musician will distinguish between the great nineteenth-century music and the poor nineteenth-century music. When he does that, he comes back toward the position of the uncritical worshiper who, being familiar with so much nineteenth-century music and so little of other periods, has felt himself left out in the cold by the young musician's enthusiasm for gawky twentieth-century tunes or somber sixteenth-century ones; he realizes that, after all, there is some common ground. There can always be conversation, and debate, and occasionally there has to be dispute, but the conversation should not lose sight of the courtesies of debate. And what is more: the mature musician finds that, as a matter of fact, when he made that generalization about nineteenth-century tunes (or whatever else he generalized about), he did not really believe it. He was only striking an attitude. He did not really hate and despise all nineteenth-century tunes. Some of them he always did like, but he could only enjoy them with a feeling of furtive guilt.

The old-fashioned and sometimes elusive virtue of sincerity is a primary asset in a minister of music. It really is forbidden to him to perform music which he is convinced is bad music, but if he finds himself making judgments which are the product either of doctrinaire attitude-striking (and therefore not really his own judgments) or which he cannot justify to a simple and nonmusical mind, then he is well advised to pull up short and revise the judgments. It is judgments that don't really spring from personal conviction, judgments that have nothing to do with any subject beyond music, that divide the company of Christians.

Church music is a pastoral matter. So if one is asked "What's *wrong* with that tune?" or "What's wrong with that custom?" one must be able to answer not only in musical terms but in human terms, from ground which is shared with the nonmusical worshiper. The musician must wrestle with the problem of relating his musical judgments to the kind of judgments that govern other church decisions. If he really feels that a certain habit, or a certain kind of music, is corrupting people's souls, or spoiling worship, or interfering with the true evangelistic work of the church, then he must say so, and he must be able to prove his point. It is simply not good enough, in this articulate age, for him either to provide what he thinks everybody wants, or to provide what he, as a musician, is sure is good music. He must combine in his judgments a sympathy with ordinary people, an inflexible professional integrity, and an ability and readiness to relate all his decisions to the overarching strategy of his church. That strategy is controlled, not by any one member or office-bearer, but by the principle that everyone brings something of his own which is valuable. Even the ignorance and prejudice of the unmusical has a value, for, where sin abounds, there grace can the more abound.

This may seem to be extracting a good deal from a single short text; it would be unwise to do it if it were not evident that this is indeed the spirit of the Gospels themselves. The church is the school of forgiveness, of interpretation and of friendship; that is what no office-bearer in the church dare forget, however committed he is to the techniques of his duty. In the Gospels themselves we find nothing, of course, about church music itself; yet we find the very heart of the matter if we are prepared to look for principles.

The great Gospel principle is, as readers will hardly need to be reminded, the Resurrection. The Resurrection is immediately preceded by the Crucifixion, but it is not extinguished by it. On the contrary, the Resurrection extinguishes the Crucifixion. But without Crucifixion there is no Resurrection. In the believer's life the translation of this is renunciation as the means to fulfillment.

At the outset one thing needs to be made clear. It is easy, but it is wrong, to make moral inferences from the faith which imply that renunciation is demanded without a promise of fulfillment, or that there was a Cross but no Resurrection. It is easy—that is the dangerous thing. Whole moral systems have been erected and enforced which lay so heavy an emphasis on renunciation as to distort the plain message of the Gospels. In music this has led to repressive and anti-aesthetic suffocation in some quarters. Renunciation in its Gospel form is the true Christian discipline. We have already said something which shows how true and practical this is. Where the musician renounces his right to be merely a musician and submits to the discipline of being a neighbor in Christ to the unmusical, he finds true fulfillment; without the discipline, if he is a church musician, he finds only division and frustration. That we have already said. But right down at the heart of music-making, or any other artistic activity, a positively ascetic renunciation is always required of the artist.[17] The discipline of creation itself is a renunciation of distracting and corrupting enthusiasms for the purpose of delivering a clear, authentic, and neighborly communication in music or in any art. No artist simply "does what he likes" when he is making a piece of work. He does that no more than a joiner does what he likes when he is making a table; as the joiner follows the grain of the wood, so the artist follows the grain of the music or the thought or the words or the lines that he has committed himself to using. The Gospel ethic is uniquely "Gospel" in that it enjoins on us a following of the "grain" of life and promises as an end-product fulfillment and happiness.

But when "renunciation" becomes corrupt and distorted, it degenerates into a means of keeping other people in subjection for one's own convenience. "The Gentiles lord it over one another." Renunciation becomes what you demand of your neighbor according to a pattern that exempts you from it.

Some religious sects have applied a form of renunciation in music which one is bound to respect, and which one can respect because of the musical quality of its end products. That seems to be true of the "vintage" English Puritans, who produced their psalm tunes, and it is surely also true of the American Mennonites, whose prohibition of organs has led to such admirable congregational part-singing and whose traditional aloofness from contemporary secular musical developments has preserved a very fine heritage of folk hymnody. It was true of the Pope's Chapel in the sixteenth century which demanded, and used, the music of Palestrina, disciplined, unaccompanied, severe. In a wider sense, indeed, the best of church music is always an illustration of the acceptance of discipline and renunciation imposed by circumstances which an artist could easily feel tempted to despise or ignore.

This is quite different from the repressive attitude to the musician which prevails in some quarters; it too often seems that "religion" is thought of as giving the philistines a license to enslave the artists. All through its history (as we said in our opening chapters) the church has been vigilant against secular corruptions in music, but sometimes, both in official pronouncements and in local attitudes, it has been ham-handed in its application of principles about which it ought to have been uneasy. It is difficult to regard the prohibition of the piano in worship and the preference for the harmonium in small buildings, enjoined in a papal declaration of 1903, as anything better than the expression of a very temporary and partial musical opinion. And when it comes to the current question of whether a guitar should be permitted in church, it is beside the point simply to claim that the guitar is not a religious instrument in the sense in which the organ is a religious instrument. On the contrary, some of the "harps" of which we read in the Old and New Testaments were a good deal more like guitars than like the romantic instrument we see adorning the modern orchestra. (The Greek word commonly translated "harp" in the Epistles is *cithara*—etymologically a first cousin of *guitar*). The question to be asked is whether *this* guitar is going to be played well, and whether it is the best instrument for the purpose to which it is going to be put. To sing a Sydney Carter song or a John Jacob Niles folk carol with a guitar is obviously right in the same sense in which it would be obviously wrong to sing it with an organ. It is not Christian renunciation to say guitars are irreligious just because they are often abused in secular life (as though Segovia had never lived). It is Christian renunciation to ensure that *this* guitar will be properly and appropriately played.

Again—picking up another point we have just made—it is not Christian renunciation to forbid all music written in the romantic era from church worship just because the romantic era produced a humanistic attitude to music and some very bad music as well. It is a Christian renunciation in the musician to ignore his prejudices and to judge music objectively on its merits and practically on its appropriateness to the need he is employed to fill. It is not even a particularly impressive "renunciation" that ties some Lutherans to chorales written before about 1715, or some English Methodists to hymns written by Charles Wesley, or some Southern Baptists to gospel songs. Any practice that dismisses whole classes of music from consideration is not renunciation but security-seeking; it leads straight to snobbery and exclusiveness and to the dreadful highbrow amateurism of the pseudopuritan.

The trouble has often been that certain kinds of theology (often but not always accurately associated with the name of Calvin) have led people to distrust too much their own humanity. The judgment that any normal person makes about music is not necessarily to be discounted when that person is in church. Therefore if a man likes "Onward, Christian soldiers," my duty as a church musician is, if I do not like it, to find out just why he does, and to see whether he is not in possession of something which I could learn from. I am bound to say that there are not nearly so many hymns which I should nowadays write off as unusable as there were when I was twenty years younger. There are certainly some. I think that "The old rugged cross" is a monstrous blasphemy, but I can give my reason, which is theological. I believe it to be wrong, misleading, and spiritually wicked to treat the Cross as affectionately as that lyric does. I believe there is all the difference in the world between that lyric and the old Latin hymn, "Faithful cross, above all other, one and only noble Tree," and that the difference is fatal. But even so, I do not regard myself as having come to the end of the evidence; I may yet learn that with all its unspeakable vulgarity it has said something authentic to somebody. I mention it as an extreme case—you will have to work mighty hard to convince me that I am wrong about it. But you may do it yet. In the matter of "Onward, Christian soldiers," which many people of high reputation have said is a very bad tune, I can find no musical fault in it whatever, and a judicious selection from its rather naïve verses still makes a hymn which, carefully used, can contribute something to the friendly company of Christians at worship. Doctrinaire criticism is not renunciation; it is repression.

One thing that our Lord did specifically invite us to renounce is any association between worship and status symbols. Of this we hear in the early verses of Matthew 6, where he compared true Christian prayer with the ostentatious and self-conscious religious exercises of the Pharisees. It may sound so odd as to be almost fanciful that a man should hire a trumpeter to call the neighborhood's attention to the fact that he was at his prayers, but a church musician knows that there is nothing fanciful about it. My very wise friend, the Rev. T. C. Micklem, went on record some years ago as saying to a conference of church musicians, "When your choir sings, you should hope that people coming into your church will say, not, 'What a good choir they've got,' but 'What a good God they've got.'" That is the truth in an epigram. It is perhaps more relevant nowadays in the United States than in Britain to ask how much expenditure on massive organs and choir accouterments is traceable to an anxiety lest the church that has these things shall lose status in its neighbors' eyes if it is without these things. The compilation of impressive music programs may indeed be a function of the church's worship, but it can be a public-relations enterprise. Certainly there are places in Britain where to sing carols at Passiontide instead of a Passion cantata would be regarded as something of a descent from eminence and as liable to forfeit public esteem.

The privacy of true prayer—which in Matthew 6 does not deny the validity of public intercession, but only that of ostentatious personal religiosity—is rather specially a musician's secret. Nine tenths of his work goes unnoticed. In the same place from which I took the quotation in the last paragraph, I myself ventured to write that the church musician's task is like that of the old medieval craftsman who for sheer delight in his work would carve, in some ancient European cathedral, some exquisite pattern, or some captivating little angel or even devil, in some dark corner eighty feet above the floor where nobody in five hundred years might ever see it.[18] But he was not wasting his time, because the same love that went into that unseen carving went also into the work that every eye could see. If the organist really does read every hymn before he plays it—the previous day if possible—if every choirmaster takes real trouble to see that what is done is done appropriately, if every chorister puts all his technical skill into the corporate rendering of the chosen anthem—who will know it? Only a fellow musician. But if love goes into the details, it will be evident in the design. If it is evident only in the design, it will be not love but self-gratification. The fact that only a musician detects the difference between a shoddy performance and a good one is no excuse whatever for leaving the details unchecked.

My justification for giving these examples of what I should call Gospel-practice in church music is that I am quite convinced of their Gospel-authenticity. Wherever you touch the Gospels, this is the emphasis that you are bound to find: discipline, leading to personal and corporate happiness. Music is meant to adorn and express and enhance true Christian happiness. The Christian must pass through the regeneration of the Cross to achieve it. But he knows what the seven deadly sins are, and he knows who has shown him how to defeat them and make them powerless. Since he is in the service of that Savior, the keynote of his music will be victory; discipline will be necessary to that, but in the end subordinate to it. After the strife, the songs of Zion.

8
A Practical Interpolation
on Teaching Unfamiliar Music

I have been asked so often what methods there are for teaching unfamiliar hymns (or other music) to a congregation that I feel it may be doing somebody a service if I make some observations about this. I do it here because what I have to say arises naturally out of what we were saying a few pages back in comment on I Corinthians 14.

Every hymnal contains some unfamiliar hymns. When there is a change of hymnal, the hymnal contains many, but even when it has been in use ten or fifteen years, even when a new one is due, the hymnal in use in any church contains some unfamiliar material, something that that congregation as a whole does not know. The musician or the minister may at any time wish to bring one of these unfamiliar pieces into use. What can he do that is consistent with that maintenance of fellowship with the unmusical to which we have referred and on which we must insist?

In the United States the admirable custom is that every member of the congregation has a hymnal with tunes to use in church. Would that this prevailed among the parsimonious British! But although it makes things much easier for those who can read music, it does not entirely meet the difficulties of learning new music for congregational use. Even if a man is musical, he takes some time to integrate a new hymn into his canon of religious "folk song"; to be able to assimilate and enjoy a new tune at once requires a good deal more musicianship than the mere ability to read a melody, and even in these educated days we cannot expect that in any but a tiny minority in our congregations.

If it is so for the musical, it is far worse for those who have little or no music. We have regretfully to write off the positively tone-deaf; the musician, by definition, can do nothing for them. The pastor (or the pastor within the musician) must encourage the tone-deaf to get all they can from the words of the hymns. But for the less-than-half musical majority, the force that the pastor and musician have to face fairly is the sense of being shortchanged, as we expressed it before. This is the resentful feeling that they are being asked to do what the church is not entitled to ask them to do—to *learn* music. That's not what the church is there for. You could put it this way: to such people, hymns are part of what they bring with them to church (I Cor. 14:26 again), rather than part of what the church offers them. Learning a new hymn places them at a disadvantage (and therefore seems to them a divisive activity) and takes up time which is better used by the church for what they think are the church's proper duties.

That is a point of view. It is legitimate only if it is not exaggerated, but the musician must not think it is always perverse. On the contrary, it can be perfectly valid. He must show cause why the congregation at large should be bothered to learn new hymns. It may be axiomatic to him, but to them it is highly questionable. Therefore before we have discussed methods at all we must advise that the musician prepare his case very well, that he be able to show at the outset why he believes the worshiper is going to be glad he took this amount of trouble and suffered this amount of distraction from the church's central concerns.

What methods are there for teaching new hymns? We can dismiss outright the notion that it is legitimate to ask a congregation to sing without notice a hymn which we are sure they will not know. Far better let them hear it sung and concentrate on the words, than make them stand and stumble their way through. It will do them no good at all. Because it is sung by hardly any, it is not a congregational hymn at that moment.

Ways of teaching new music can be divided between indirect and direct methods, the indirect method is to use some means of making a tune familiar without involving the congregation in any special act of attention; direct methods are those in which the congregation is faced immediately with the demand to learn and sing. Indirect methods include

1. the use of hymn-tune preludes by the organist, and
2. the use of hymn-anthems by the choir, together with possibly
3. the singing of the new hymn as an anthem.

Hymn-tune preludes abound. I must say that I regard most of the modern ones as very strictly utility music. Sometimes they are good music, but often when they are too allusive and clever to be particularly useful for our present purpose. There is a very useful list of hymn-tune preludes in the *Companion to the Hymnal (1940)*; organists' societies are capable of amplifying this and keeping it up to date.

But even so, there may not be a hymn-tune prelude on the tune you have in mind, and when the prelude is allusive and esoteric, when indeed it does anything more interesting that producing a descant to a prominently placed rendering of the tune itself, it will not serve this purpose. Since your new tune may well be a tune recently composed, one way and another you will be fairly lucky if you find what you need in this area.

Hymn-anthems are, heaven knows, a somewhat lowly form of church music. They are desperately easy to compose. But here there are some composers who have made it their business to write hymn-anthems on tunes which may well be in the practice repertory of contemporary American congregations—especially revived folk hymns. The choir-master may easily be able to help here, but again, the composition needs to be sufficiently "obvious" to catch attention if it is to have any pedagogic value.

Frankly, the approach I should recommend is the third —the use of the hymn itself as a choir-anthem. Had I charge of an organ and choir now, I should make a point of capitalizing on what I have just called the dangerous ease with which hymn-tune anthems can be composed. I should compose them. This is not a formidable assignment at all, if taken reasonably lightly. I should get the choir thoroughly familiar with the tune; then I should assign different verses to different sections (one for unison men, one for unison women, one unaccompanied, one perhaps with the lower parts hummed and the upper part sung, one full unison with a varied accompaniment). I should devise four-bar or eight-bar interludes between verses, and there would be your hymn-anthem. What is important is this: I should almost certainly throw it all away when the end had been reached—when the congregation knew the hymn well. The highly trained organists and choirmasters who abound in American churches ought to be able to accomplish what is so confidently recommended by an amateur; if they cannot, they ought to be trained to do it as part of their academic courses. This kind of "disposable music" can be exceedingly effective, so long as nobody feels that he is bound to get it published. And the strategy is good because the pedagogy is still discreetly hidden. A congregation of average stupidity might easily be aroused to prejudice against a choir singing where they expected to sing themselves, or against the plain rendering of a hymn instead of the kind of anthem they are used to. In the long run one would hope that this nonsense would be dissipated, but as a practical step, applicable now, what is here recommended could be both acceptable and effective.

But sooner or later the direct approach has to be faced. In this you have no choices beyond these three:

4. teaching a hymn to the people outside worship but in church—that is, at an arranged "congregational practice";

5. teaching it to them outside worship and outside church—that is, at some fellowship gathering;

6. teaching it as part of worship.

The commonly recommended course in Britain seems to be the first of these. There are many objections to it, which apply equally to the second. A new hymn is to be used in the worship of the whole congregation. At any specially convened meeting for practice you will not see the whole congregation. It may be that you will see only the musical. This may be the best that can be managed, and undoubtedly something is achieved if a fair number of people come to the service knowing the "new" hymn. They can to some extent pull the rest along with them. And a keen group can be taught better and with greater goodwill than a generalized congregation. The real difficulty is to find the right time for such a practice and the right frequency. In most people's experience, if the congregational practice is a separate meeting, sufficient frequency to make a real impact on the repertory may kill the meetings by reducing the attendance to a very small number; while the calling of such practice meetings for, say, half an hour before a Sunday service, apart from administrative difficulties, will quite certainly attract only a small fraction of the congregation if it is repeated too often.

One wonders, therefore, whether there is not something to be said for the bold and perhaps irreverent suggestion that a time for hymn-singing be occasionally, but regularly, interpolated within the worship itself. Once again the unfortunate anthem may have to give ground. Could the time used for the performance of an anthem (or two anthems in opulent places) be used for congregational praise of this special kind? This does not mean that the practice should be intruded into the service at the point where the anthem is expected; it simply means using those bonus minutes for this purpose.

This is best achieved if with perfect regularity, say on one Sunday each month, a section of the service is given to "praise"; this need not mean only learning a new hymn. It may include the instruction of the congregation in how to sing an old hymn well. The new hymn can be prepared by "indirect methods" during the previous Sunday or two; it can also be prepared by a few minutes spent bringing a tired old veteran hymn to life. Again, a choirmaster ought to be equipped with the necessary know-how to do this; if he is not, something was lacking in his training.

But is this an unwarrantable interference with worship? That depends on what you think worship is. Taken near the beginning of a service, this kind of instruction in the right hands can be a positive act of fellowship. It can help the congregation not merely with the specific business of learning a new hymn, but to understand what the musical part of the service is there to do, how hymns are chosen, and above all what the force of the words, as well as the tunes, is when hymns are sung. Some may object that the restlessness or musical sales talk on such an occasion is incompatible with the spirit of worship. If such a suggestion were made to me, I should ask why this is assumed to be so. There are certain inhibiting notions of "reverence" which seem to me to have more to do with primitive Old-Testament taboo than with the gospel. But I should also wish to ensure that the music session was very carefully prepared by whoever was in charge of it. Any unnecessary talk, any losing of the place, any wasting of time, anything short of the highest professional standards in communication, would be out of place.

The real advantage of this method is, I think, that without too much fuss and sense of crisis it builds music-making into the fabric of worship and fellowship, which is what we are really aiming to do. Satisfactory results are never achieved so long as music-making is something hastily and anxiously added to the structure; it wants to be part of the structure. In other words, we want the man in the congregation to say, not, "This is what they make us do," but "This is what we do"; we want that to be said of hymn practice as naturally as it can be said of public prayer and Bible-reading.

One other method of hymn promotion must be mentioned: this is what the Lutherans especially are making familiar just now under the name "the Hymn of the Week program." This is something outside the immediate control of local directors. It is a denomination-wide project depending on the old-fashioned and admirable habit of singing hymns at home. The American Lutheran Church has prepared a schedule of sixty-two hymns (one hymn for each week plus ten hymns for special festivals), issued a booklet of their words and music, and prepared sumptuously produced LP records on which all sixty-two hymns are performed, and encourages the faithful in this way to establish a "canon" of sixty-two hymns that will be known to everybody; all are chosen from the current *Service Book and Hymnal* (1958), and among some familiar ones are included many that will be either wholly new or new in the version given. This is ambitious and can be done economically only by a large denomination. But behind it there is the encouragement of domestic hymn-singing, and this is a point that can be made anywhere. It is probably true that the problem of the new hymn simply did not exist in the late nineteenth century, because families sang hymns round the piano or domestic organ on Sundays, and as a matter of course knew everything that their hymnals printed. There is no reason in the world why we should not still ask our people to have hymnals of their own and use them other than in church worship, even if the sociologists rush in to tell us that the family has disappeared as a social unit.

Once again we are back at I Corinthians 14:26. If the worshiper brings his hymns with him, there is no problem. To some extent he must take the responsibility, if the singing of hymns, and especially of unfamiliar ones, has come to be something which the church seems to impose on him. If he brought his own, there would be no need. But the situation is as it is, and such means of combining efficiency, worship, and friendliness as any minister of music can use, let him use, and good luck to him.

III
THE CHURCH MUSICIAN
AND WORSHIP

9
The Art of Worship

In a forthcoming companion book to this one, one on words, music, and the church, I will venture to make some suggestions concerning the nature of public worship which I shall not repeat here, except to say that the central point is that worship is a kind of drama. I do not mean drama considered as entertainment, and therefore I do not by saying this in any way want to imply approval of gimmicks and personal techniques of advertisement such as have sometimes disfigured public worship in our time. I mean rather that in the sense that the Last Supper was a drama, the Lord's Supper is a drama. The Last Supper was a drama in which our Lord said "Do this" (and "drama" is a Greek word meaning "that which is done"); it was also a drama in the sense that in doing something he was implying something within it and beyond it; his action was symbolic—and so is our action meant to be. And since all Christian worship derives from the Lord's Supper and gathers round it and finds its consummation in it, there is an element of drama in all Christian worship. I mention this here because I want to connect it with certain things I have already said, and also to derive from it one or two points directly relevant to the church musician's work.

If I may speak personally, and as a nonpracticing musician to musicians who are going about their daily musiness, I would ask them to compare their work with mine. I am what is called in the United States a "preacher." About the activity of preaching I have a certain conviction. I do not believe that the preacher's object in preaching is what it is sometimes claimed to be, still less what people who know nothing about it represent it to be.

Some people think his business is to impress people with his own brilliance. That is obviously absurd. Others think that he hopes people will remember everything he said. That is wildly unpractical; he would insist on their taking notes if he thought of himself as a lecturer. Others think he is there to teach people what they did not know before; there is something terrifying about the thought of a teaching course that lasts the whole of one's life. Others again think he is there to answer people's moral questions and solve their problems, to which one must reply that to stand up in front of two hundred people and hope to answer the moral problems of each one in the space of twenty (or even forty) minutes is a wonderfully inefficient way of setting about that process.

All these views are, I think, attributing to the preacher purposes which are properly served by other office-bearers, or by himself in other capacities. Leaving aside self-advertisement, the need for information is properly served by the catechist, the need for comment on current affairs by the journalist, and the need for moral advice by the counselor. The minister may have to be all these things to his people, but he is not doing any of those things when he is preaching in the course of public worship.

My own view is this: when I have preached a sermon I do not chiefly hope that any given person in the congregation will have thought it a good sermon, although I shall do what I can to make it a good one; I do not hope that any given person will remember everything, or even much, that I said. But I do most firmly and fervently hope that somebody will go out of church saying, whether he remembers anything I said or not, "Now I can go home and get that difficult letter written." "Now I can go and patch up that quarrel." "Now I can believe that what is now hidden from me will be shown." My own prayer is that God the Holy Spirit will turn my words into something else. I don't want him to leave them just as they were, in anybody's mind. I want him to turn them into a decision. The difference between my view of preaching and that which I am afraid I find myself opposing might be put this way: that the other kind of preacher sees the symbolic response to his sermon in people coming toward him. I see it in people turning their backs on me, going out of the church door, and getting hold

107

of whatever difficulty it was that before they came in was too much for them. If I conducted an evangelistic service (well, to be candid, I think I always do!) I should want people to register decisions by emptying the building, not by crowding the counselors' rooms. I recognize, of course, that we are talking about different things. In a mission to total unbelievers, I agree that my method probably would not work. But in the worship of the Christian community, in which the minister of music for whom I am writing is doing his work, that is how I see it, and how I am hoping to persuade my reader to see it. If my sermon, which comes from one voice, can be transformed by the Holy Spirit into a decision for every person present, different in every case, then I think each has heard the gospel "in his own language," and the pentecostal miracle has happened again.

This is what I would venture to call the "dramatic" theory of preaching. It is not saying that the preacher is a film star. It is saying that words can be transformed into agents of personal decision. What actually happens, so far as we can analyze it at all, seems to be this. A person comes to worship partly because it is his habit to come, but also, if he knows his Christian business, because he knows he has a need. It is quite likely to be a specific need, and if he has cultivated that self-awareness which is the Christian's answer to the psychiatrist's couch, he knows what that need is. He has no expectation that I, the preacher, will be dealing specifically with that need. But, if I do my work properly and if it is of the Lord, then through the words I say will come to that person a new conviction that God loves him, that life is worth living, that the devil has been conquered and can be conquered again.

Let me be more precise. I as preacher contribute to that hoped for effect. But others contribute as well. The presence of friends at worship makes a massive contribution. And the musician makes a contribution as well.

The whole purpose of these pages is to amplify the musician's freedom through the disciplines of his faith, not to restrict it; and it seems to me that, where the musician can really feel that he works as a member of a creative team in public worship, he will find that he gains the greatest fulfillment and happiness from his work. We have hinted at the sources of division and trouble in the musical part of worship; we need to expose the secret of the highest happiness, and this is where I believe it lies.

If an act of public worship is rightly understood as a kind of drama, it is helpful to remember that drama is, no matter what the puritans may say, a thoroughly serious business. The proper communication of a playwright's message through drama depends on the close and confident teamwork of actors, producer, electricians, stagehands, publicity men and theater manager. It also depends, even when the content of the play is lightweight, on high seriousness of purpose in the author himself. Just because the content of many plays and films is trifling there is no reason to overlook the quite astonishing amount of coordinated serious work that goes into the production of a play, or a film, or a television program. The meanest of God's creatures in television (in Britain at least) are ministers of religion doing solo performances, but nobody who has done one can fail to be astonished at the number of people who seem to be seriously employed for the purpose of getting him on to the screen.

Without wishing to draw the parallel too closely between producing a "show" and administering public worship (and in the book I referred to, I hope I will clear this up to some extent), I would urge that for the proper communication of the creative word of God in worship a much closer cooperation between minister, choirmaster, organist, choir, church management, education authorities, and office-bearers is required than we normally look for. Too often—perhaps almost universally—each major participant in worship plays a solo without reference to anybody else. Tensions between ministers and organists are lamentably frequent; where they are not openly apparent they often exist in the form of resigned resentments. The only way that occurs to some ministers or musicians of relating those tensions is simply to take the line that cooperation is unnecessary anyway. Then the whole "production" falls flat, and people wonder why this has happened. Alternatively, one of the participants "steals the show" or "hogs the scene," and because it is all in a religious context perhaps the unfortunate loser in this unlovely contest will say that this is the Lord's will and keep quiet about it. All of which is very much to the detriment of public worship, or, at all events, it means that opportunities are being lost.

For example: a minister may regard it as his duty to prescribe the hymns to be sung in a service. I do myself, now that I am a pastor. But when I was an organist, I knew the difference between the minister who prescribed hymns with some thought of the congregation, and the minister who prescribed them with no thought, or with inadequate imagination. My business as an organist happened to be in a college chapel in which most preachers were visitors. I used to say somewhat irreverently that I could predict the quality of the preaching from the praise list which had been sent to me in advance. I was rarely wrong. It was easy to see whether the minister had jammed down the numbers of the first four hymns that came into his head, or whether he was choosing hymns because he personally liked them, or whether (such men scored very low marks when they appeared before the congregation) they were going to treat our student congregation as "young people." There were also the good men who knew what they were doing—and who took the trouble to find out, or imagine, what *we* were doing. I can recall one specific pair of successive Sundays on which the praise lists overlapped with respect to a certain very well-known hymn, and I vividly remember how badly it "went" on the second occasion and how inspiringly on the first. The difference corresponded exactly to the difference between a preacher who had the virtue of being able to understand what he sounded like to the congregation, and the preacher who was simply "giving a solo."

Holding as I do that the minister in a Reformed church is responsible for the "libretto" of a service, for the "script" of the play, I am sure he should choose the congregational hymns; but he is a simpleton if he does not either know, or take the trouble to find out, which hymns the congregation finds acceptable and which it finds difficult, which communicate and which do not communicate, which will evoke the response he wants and which will not. How greatly his minister of music can help him—especially if the musician is (as he is so often in the U.S.A.) not the organist. He can sense, and if he knows his business remember, what hymns have what effect on the congregation, point out where the minister has miscalculated, (if American hymnals were sanely printed) rescue a difficult hymn by suggesting a change of tune, interpret the congregation to the minister.

But so many ministers of music are not interested in hymns. Perhaps they would be more so if they saw them as part of a "sacred script," having important dramatic value as audience participation. Perhaps they would like hymns more if they liked people more. The minister of music who lets his minister of the gospel down by having no views and no representative part to play ought to mend his ways or leave his appointment.

Again: the minister of music may well regard it as his business to plan the choir music. If he has read the earlier part of this book he may perhaps have some uneasiness about the role of the choir in a modern reformed service anyway. But he ought in any case to have questions about the relevance of the choir's traditional anthems. What are they doing in the "script" of this dramatic act? Have they the virtue of spontaneity, or the virtue of planned relevance?

It may well be too much to ask that the anthems for a service be chosen from their texts: practical difficulties may get in the way. But if the minister and the musician plan things cooperatively, it ought to be reasonably easy to plan the anthems according to the season of the church's year, or according to a series of subjects.

I myself would go further, but in doing so I may well not take the majority of my readers with me. I am sure that there are some anthems which in themselves are eloquent sermons. For the sake of letting them speak with a full voice, I would cheerfully remodel the service so as to give them a well-prepared and conspicuous place. One such anthem is the magnificent "Greater love hath no man," by John Ireland. I simply would not want to preach a full-length sermon after hearing that; I would want only to prepare the way for it to speak, through scriptural words and fine music, to the congregation. Once one has accepted the dramatic principle in worship, the alteration of order, the shift of emphasis from verbal preaching in one service to prayer in another, to music in a third, to Bible-reading in a fourth, can be delicately managed with immense profit to a congregation, and, I suspect, with an equally great sense of freshness and encouragement in the musicians.

Now in the U.S.A. there are opportunities for developing thoughts of this kind far more ample than any which exist in Britain. In my own country all we can do is experiment with slender resources. In the U.S.A. there are already establishments associated with seminaries in which church music is being taught. I am obliged to repeat what I have ventured to say more than once before, that here is the real place of dialogue between music and theology, and therefore the field of development of truly theological and truly dramatic worship. It would be a magnificent thing if in some adventurous seminary a creative theologian and a group of creative musicians sat down together to talk about a new kind of worship, with a professional producer of drama sitting in. The campus chapels of the U.S.A. could be powerhouses of a new kind of evangelism. It would, on my hypothesis, be somewhat different from what we normally mean by evangelism. But it is the answer, I am sure, to the mounting anxieties of the nonfundamentalist communions.

What might our "new theologians" have achieved in our generation if they had had an artist among them! What may the best of them yet achieve if they can interest a musician in what they are trying to say. It is hardly too much to claim that if it won't sing, it isn't good theology. On that basis I sometimes dream of what might have happened had Paul Tillich got together with a musician and a dramatist, or of what may happen if somebody as eager for communication as he was and as intellectually devout succeeds in doing so yet.

But we must not leave it to the distinguished and the dead. The teamwork between music and theology can be begun wherever there is a gathered congregation, a musician, and a minister. It will probably begin with repentance on the part of any who hoped that their office would protect them from the demands of teamwork, and go on to a sense of discovery and fellowship. But in the end my conviction is that the gospel will flash out again with a force the greater because it comes from an unexpected generation if we can learn this lesson of cooperation between minister and musician, accepting the basic fact that whether they knew it or not, both are artists.

Therefore, to end our conversation on a practical note, I want to suggest one or two ways in which, if there is this cooperation between minister and organist, worship can be transformed. They are based on experiments which have in fact been put into action in a church whose musical appointments are rudimentary, but which had during the time of their operation an organist of distinction. They are designed to show what can be done without waiting for massive musical facilities; they may, exported to the United States, carry with them a touch of judgment on those establishments whose musical appointments are so lavish that the musicians would think these proceedings not worth their choirs' trouble. That I cannot help, and anyhow they can be amplified. But—consider:

1. *The use of the Bible in worship.* It occurred to me one day after I had occupied my pastorate for four years that I had never preached from a text in the book of Job. Examining the cause of this I traced it to the restrictions of our order of service, which provided for the usual twenty-verse reading of Scripture. How can you possibly read twenty verses from Job? Here is a religious drama which makes no kind of sense unless it is heard right through. Along with this, it occurred to me that we are now in almost a medieval situation; the public reading of Scripture in the Middle Ages was instituted for the benefit of people who could not read for themselves. Well, I said, we will institute a public reading of Scripture on the grand scale for those who won't read for themselves. So we read the book of Job.

I took down James Moffatt's translation of Job (which I think easily the finest) and edited it in four large sections, to be read by different readers using different parts of the church, in four successive morning services. The readings occupied a quarter of an hour or so each, instead of the prescribed three or four minutes. I enlisted the help of good readers from the congregation. (We have no public address system in our church; this is a blessing, because it means that whoever speaks must take the trouble to speak audibly, but given that, you do not have always to speak from the place where the microphone is fixed. Public address systems are death to contemporary worship of most kinds.)

But it was necessary to see that the congregation left the church at their usual time; you cannot suddenly hold your congregation a quarter of an hour beyond the accustomed time of closure without incurring the charge of being arrogantly thoughtless. This meant retiming the rest of the service. It meant planning fairly carefully to see that hymns and prayers said what was required, but said it economically. The ample reading made a short sermon easy to achieve. Time taken for intimations was saved by having these printed on the orders of service.

That was a beginning. It has, in fact, become a custom which we keep up on the opening Sundays of the year. We have in this way read dramatically the stories of Joseph and of Jacob, and most recently we read that of Jeremiah, using passages from the prophecy alternating with passages from the law and the books of Kings.

Musically this made no demands on us; the congregation's response was in carefully chosen hymns. Had there been an anthem provided for in the service it would have either had to be scrapped or substituted for one of the hymns, and it would have had to be very carefully selected. But in the Jeremiah series we did illustrate with the reading, and on one occasion the singing, of psalms; that is where a choir might have given some valuable help. (We used a soloist and the Grail version of the Psalter.)

On another occasion—this was many years ago, but I have had the temerity to repeat it—being at a loss to know what to do with the second service of harvest thanksgiving, I thought we might read the whole of the book of Ruth. There are several ways of doing this—one voice per chapter, or assigning different voices to different parts. (But in any reading of this kind, if I may offer this advice, don't make the mistake of producing this preposterous effect—

Voice 1: Then Naomi her mother-in-law said to her
Voice 2: My daughter, should I not seek a house with you. . . .

Either give the whole passage to one reader or rewrite the whole affair omitting the speech introductions—

Naomi: My daughter, should I not seek . . .)

The four chapters were separated on one occasion by the singing of psalms, on another by the singing of unusual hymns set to easy congregational tunes. The content of the mini-sermon was, of course, the implications of the very last verse of the book. Then—"Hail to the Lord's anointed: great David's greater Son."

There is more than one way of making a congregation free of the Bible; the need to hear the Bible in really large sections is great. Split up into three-minute readings and half-verse texts, it loses three quarters of its power and ninety percent of its humanity. Above all, it is the Old Testament that gains from this treatment. Only the customary sacredness of "orders of service" prevents this. The musical demands can be absolutely minimal, and the "production" difficulties are confined to the selection of good readers; there is no need for people to learn their lines. But with enterprising and ample musical resources, how much more can be done than that!

2. *The use of the choir in worship.* We do not sing an anthem at every service, but occasionally the director of music takes over, and the choir prepares a series of anthems around which a service is constructed. This is a very flexible technique and can be very rewarding. The easiest thing to do is to combine anthems with Bible readings in an exposition of the gospel through the traditional seasons of the Christian year. Or a theme can be chosen, and anthems from various periods in various styles can be chosen to illustrate it, and arranged to form a shapely act of worship using also Bible readings and hymns.

But we discovered one unexpected thing when we tried this. Our music director conceived the idea of educating the choir and congregation by arranging four evening services featuring anthems of different periods. There was a sixteenth-century service, then a J. S. Bach service, then a nineteenth-century service, and finally a twentieth-century service. I was a little frightened by this. I wonder if it would not be too pedagogic. The choir was not there to give courses in music history. What about my unmusical friend whom I must always keep in mind?

I had reckoned without church history. The interesting thing was that the anthems, grouped by centuries, grouped themselves also by subjects. Anthems of which our small choir was capable turned out to produce their own "subjects" when arranged in groups. The sixteenth-century musicians in their short anthems tended to make settings of prayers from the English Prayer Book. J. S. Bach had his pietist fervor. The nineteenth-century men used Scripture. The twentieth-century composers used semi-secular literature of a high quality, and showed some exegetical sense. So each service turned out to be homogeneous, and the series achieved a pleasing balance of emphases. There was no sermon in these services; the "exposition" consisted in the juxtaposition of anthems with readings and hymns, and enough information was given on the orders of service to put the congregation "in the picture."

This will be recognized as essentially a development on the "lessons and carols" technique, and I would certainly commend the use of lessons-and-carols services for seasons other than Christmas.[19]

3. *The use of literature in worship.* This is not a strictly musical point, but I mention it because it was my own music director who suggested it to me. People won't, we said, read their Bibles. But my experience is that they won't read anything serious to any considerable extent. Personally I am not much given to quotation in the course of sermons. Unless the quotation is at the highest pitch of wit and brevity, I doubt if it has any effect beyond assuring the congregation how well read I am. Yet on the other hand, why should the congregation be confined to my own store of wisdom, which heaven knows is meager enough? Are there not great things in the poets, or even the theologians, which they might be glad to hear? Is not there occasionally something written well, memorably, topically, in some periodical that they would not see, but that says just what will help them?

I found it possible to devise a service in which, on a given subject, there would be a reading from Scripture and a reading from a modern source (the source might be anything from *Piers Plowman* to *The Times*). An address could be given that would keep things in due proportion, and I certainly would not touch the idea of substituting any modern literature for the Bible. The difficulty here is to find anything in modern literature, poetry apart, which is short enough to make sense without prolixity, and good enough literature to stand public reading. Therefore this is not a thing I would undertake to do often. But there is no reason in the world why, if I am allowed to quote in the pulpit, I should not read more extensively from the pulpit. I happen to believe that it is a Christian's duty to read, if he can, good literature and to keep in touch, if he can, with contemporary thought by reading newspapers carefully and not frivolously; the church can set an example.

4. *The use of illustrative Scriptures in worship.* By this

cumbersome subheading I mean to distinguish the kind of worship which uses a great deal of Bible reading but selects readings from many parts to illustrate a central theme. This needs to be done with the greatest care, for it is fatally easy to indulge in typologies which the Scriptures were not designed to sustain. Knowing these dangers, I have not myself attempted it. But as an example of how it can be done with small resources and without much preparation, I wish to quote in full a service which was held in the Congregational church in Dewsbury, a Yorkshire manufacturing town. It happens to be relevant to state that this service was conceived ten days before it was held; this I happen to know because it was my own failure to visit this church as its anniversary preacher that created the emergency out of which it arose. Never, I think, was a minister more profitably withheld from doing his duty. The service is based on the story of Noah, and was clearly created by somebody who knew Benjamin Britten's *Noye's Fludde*.[20] But it uses perfectly normal church-service material. If the reader cares to go through it with a copy of the Scriptures, he will get the feel of it at once.

THE ARK: FESTIVAL SERVICE AT DEWSBURY, 19 July 1965
             Minister: the Reverend Robert W. Courtney
Sentences: Psalm 118 verses 19-20
HYMN: "Open now thy gates of beauty"
Prayer of Adoration and Confession
Collection and Prayer of Dedication

———

Reading: The story of Noah
                Genesis 6:9-11, 13-14, 17-18, 22; 7:11b-12, 17-18, 21;
                8:1-4, 15-16; 9:1
Psalm 93 (92, Grail Version) "The Lord is King," music by
        Gélineau
Narrator: Noah lived in a world shaking to its foundations. Take
        his story as a race memory of disaster in the Euphrates
        valley, or as simply as you please: but in his world
        there was safety for none—save for those who righteously and obediently lived as God's people. In sudden
        disaster, when men least expected peril, there was a
        refuge for those who trusted God.
Reader: Matthew 24:37-39
Action: Entrance of Noah and family. They build the Ark. When
        it is finished, they stand as in prayer.

117

Reader: Genesis 7:15-16

HYMN: "Eternal Father, strong to save"

Reading: Genesis 8:15; 9:1*b*
Noah's family leave the Ark.

Narrator: So then the pattern for God's people was established—that they should have a place of refuge—an ark to bear them through the years of storm—the little company, and then the nation, who survived the crash of empires and the years of desolation. They might come in and shelter—but God would send them out again, to be fruitful and multiply and fill the earth—to bring all creation to God.

Anthem: "O Lord, I will praise thee" (Gordon Jacob)

Narrator: Then came the time when, enslaved and nearly overwhelmed in a foreign land, all the hope of God's people lay in a little reed boat among the bulrushes of the Nile—no bigger than a basket for a baby. And from this Ark there sprang such a man as led Israel out and through the waters of the Sea: with God as refuge and deliverer, that they should praise his name and declare his doings among the people.

Action: Moses enters, carrying the Books of the Law, goes up into the Ark.

Reader: Exodus 19:4-6*a*

Narrator: So through the years the floods lifted up their voice; the waters lifted up their thunder; but greater than the roar of mighty waters, more glorious than the surging of the sea, the Lord is glorious on high.

———

Reader: Matthew 24:37-39

HYMN: "Fierce raged the tempest"

Action: Entrance of Christ and disciples. They pause in the area in front of the Ark.

Reader: Mark 4:35-36
They enter the boat.

Narrator: Mark 4:37-41
Christ rises to rebuke the storm.

Reader: Matthew 28:18*b*-20

Narrator: "Go forth therefore and make all nations my disciples; and be assured, I am with you always to the end of time." Out they went to be persecuted and harried—but then on the walls of Greek settlements and Roman towns men saw signs appear that brought comfort and courage to the little Christian church: the sign of the fish, whose letters spelled out "Jesus Christ, Son of God, Savior"—the monogram of Christ's name—and the boat, the Galilean fishing boat, the Ark with the Cross—symbol of God's people under his protection.

Action: Enter two Christians from the early church. One keeps watch while the other chalks up the symbol on a wall. They then take ropes hanging from the Ark and use them to raise the mast—which is a Cross. They secure it.

Solo: "Begone, unbelief" (verse 1)

Narrator: Now again the world darkens around us and the foundations are shaken. Not now the thunder clouds and lightning flashes are our fear, but the clouds that tower and mushroom; the silent, invisible, deadly tides that may lap the earth. And with them the cold winds of unbelief and the chill knowledge that men have lost their direction, and many their purpose.

Reader: Matthew 24:37-39, 42

Action: Family at breakfast table: Father, Mother, and two children.

    Mother: Buck up, John, you'll be late.

    John: 'S all right: bags of time. Say, Mum, can you get some more of these things (lifts packet of breakfast cereal)—there's a —

    Father: Eat your breakfast! What are you doing this afternoon, Susan?

    Susan: Baths again.

    Father: You ought to be a fish: all comes of your mother being a mermaid.

    Mother: Oh, shut up, Bill—and what about the reading, or the children *will* be late.

    Father: (reads I Peter 3: 14-21*a*). Let us pray. . . . They rise, and all rise with them for

HYMN: "Lord Jesus, think on me"

During the singing the cast take the places they occupy for the rest of the service, and the serving deacons lay the Table.

Minister: Revelation 21:1

Prayers

"Lift up your hearts"

Breaking of Bread and delivery of the Elements.

Prayer

Hymn: "From glory to glory Advancing"

Benediction

This service uses the simplest forms of narration, together with subtle yet boldly drawn lines of biblical typology. The ear and perception of the participating congregation, caught by the picturesque story of Noah, is firmly fixed to the

119

conception of storm, strife, and the Hebrew notion of the Flood. The hymns "Eternal Father," "Fierce raged the tempest," and "Lord Jesus, think on me" develop the theme, providing congregational emphasis at the turning points. The solo reinforces this with the lines

> with Christ in the vessel
> I smile at the storm.

The harsh little piece of dialogue at the communion table links the communion through the amusing throwaway image of the fish with domesticity; the following reading at once links it with the exalted New Testament doctrine of baptism.

The thought is thus firmly anchored in the Bible, and equally firmly anchored in life. Before the congregation realizes it, the whole business has risen from the old folk tale of Noah to the splendors of the Lord's Supper through the New Testament story of redemption.

It probably needs to be said that experiments of this sort are most meaningful when they are set against a background of the normal preaching and sacramental services, but you do not get to this level unless you have detected the growing point of drama in Christian worship. I leave it there—it would be superfluous to attempt any special advice to musicians on how they could enrich and add impetus to worship in any of these forms by the judicious use of their resources.

The only other thing that is required is the willingness of the resources to be used. Here are disciplines of the spirit as well as quite strict disciplines of the aesthetic, but what a field for teamwork—what a chance to prove the practicality of Paul's advice that all may bring a psalm, an interpretation, a tongue, a revelation!

With that I close my conversation.

Perhaps the future of the church's communication with the world lies with the prophecy and priesthood of the musicians, who handle mysteries and make them friendly, who can speak the unspeakable in a language that uses no words, in whose art action and thought are joined, in whose hands applied science is the servant of beauty and honor. In every place where the gospel is being preached, this secret is waiting for its revelation.

NOTES

1. This point will be treated in greater detail in the first chapter of my forthcoming book on words, music, and the church.
2. See J. A. T. Robinson, *The New Reformation* (Philadelphia: The Westminster Press, 1965), and many recent articles in *The New Christian* (fortnightly, founded September, 1965).
3. For convenient summaries of early church views, see my book, *The Church and Music* (Naperville, Ill.: Alec R. Allenson, 1950); Oliver Strunk, ed., *Source Readings in Music History* (New York: W. W. Norton & Co., 1950); and the early chapters of any reputable music history such as the *New Oxford History of Music,* Book II, or P. H. Lang, *Music in Western Civilization* (New York: W. W. Norton & Co., 1941).
4. It is noticeable that the most notorious persecutions of Christians on record in early history took place in the reigns of Antoninus Pius (A.D. 138-61), Marcus Aurelius (161-80), Decius (249-51), and Diocletian (284-305), all of whom were, by Roman standards, men of conscience and honor, and the second of whom was a philosopher whom later Christians treated with considerable respect.
5. Anybody who travels in Wales can amuse himself by tracing the Christian history of the country through its place-names. The very common prefix "Llan" comes from the same root as "lawn" and means an enclosure—a court or quadrangle round which a group of buildings stood, or simply enclosed by an angle of one building. From that it came to mean the religious building itself—the chapel. So there is, for example, a place in Wales called *Llantrisant,* which recognizably means "community of three saints"—a tin monastery where three holy men spent their days. Llanpumpsaint similarly means "community of five saints." Llandudno means "Community of St. Tudno," and Lampeter (variations of spelling come naturally in a language spoken long before it was written) means "Community of St. Peter."
6. Recorded on Argo RG 436 (Zrg 5436).

7. See his *Ein' Feste Burg,* "A Mighty Fortress."
8. In *The English Hymnal,* still the best representative source for hymnological history, there are 104 tunes from Lutheran sources and 15 from the Genevan psalters. (The complete Genevan psalter, be it said, had 110 tunes; the collection of chorales compiled by Zahn about 1890 contains 8,806 tunes.)
9. In Tye's metrical setting of *The Acts* (about 1553); see Maurice Frost, *English and Scottish Psalms and Hymn Tunes, c. 1543-1677* (London: Oxford University Press and S.P.C.K., 1953), pp. 360-61, the second half of the music to chap. 8.
10. See R. R. Terry, *A Forgotten Psalter* (1935) and Neil Livingston's edition of the 1635 Scottish Psalter (1864).
11. See my book, *The Music of Christian Hymnody* (London: Independent Press, 1957) chapter 17 and examples 153-59.
12. "Prophets were religiously respected for their abnormal powers but socially despised for their uncouth ways, and on either ground Saul was in unexpected company." G. B. Caird, on I Samuel in *The Interpreter's Bible,* II (Nashville: Abingdon Press, 1953), 934.
13. John Skinner, ed., *Isaiah 1-39* (New York: Cambridge University Press, 1930), p. 34.
14. Artur Weiser, *The Psalms* (Philadelphia: The Westminster Press, 1962), pp. 35-52.
15. See my book, *Ascent to the Cross* (Nashville: Abingdon Press, 1962), chap. 1.
16. There is doubt, which I respect, about Paul's authorship of Ephesians. It does not in any way affect this argument.
17. *The Organist and the Congregation,* a pamphlet (London: Independent Press, 1952) containing addresses given to the first conference of Congregational Organist and Choirmasters at Mansfield College, Oxford, in July, 1951.
18. See my book, *Church Music and Theology* (Philadephia: Fortress Press, 1960), pp. 20-22.
19. For an example of a Passiontide carol service, see my book, *The English Carol* (New York: Oxford University Press, 1958), pp. 253-55.
20. A discussion of the implications of *Noye's Fludde* for contemporary worship will be included in my forthcoming book, *Words, Music, and the Church.*

INDEX OF SCRIPTURE REFERENCES

INDEX OF NAMES AND SUBJECTS